"Imagine spending *every* day of your life influencing the culture and changing the atmosphere with prayer and the gospel! Sammy Tippit's message of innovation breaks us out of isolation and into daily participation in disciple multiplication and revival preparation all over the world."

—Kathy Branzell, president, National Day of Prayer Task Force

"Throughout the history of revival, God has used technological advances to help communicate the message of hope in powerful ways. Faithfully seeking the Lord in each epoch and following His leadership, the strategic use of new technology has resulted in 'unprecedented spiritual harvest' for the Kingdom. Sammy Tippit highlights 'the biblical and historical connection between innovation and revival,' and the wisdom of prayerfully considering today's technology for the awakening of nations and the fulfillment of the Great Commission. Sammy's mission, vision, and example inspire the reader to be a 'biblical dreamer' with the Lord so that today's Christian can do greater works."

—Byron Paulus, executive director & CEO, Life Action Ministries, and founder, OneCry

"Sammy is a true pioneer in using current technology to advance the gospel in our modern era. He's learned it, applied it to reach literally millions of people for Christ, and now he is sharing with others how to do it. That's a true pioneer and disciple of Christ. I strongly recommend this book to everyone who wants to be used of God to reach our world for Christ. It's biblical, simple, and practical."

—Wade Akins, missionary with Pioneer Missions Global

"Sammy Tippit clearly describes how over the centuries God has used men and women willing to take risks. They used innovation, new technologies, and the methods of their day—whether it was the Roman roads in ancient times or the internet and social media of today—to deliver the Gospel to the masses in an effort to fulfill the Great Commission. Because Sammy is himself a risk-taker and eager to step out in faith to learn and apply new methods of sharing the Gospel with people around the world, his efforts have resulted in many thousands coming to faith in Christ and being discipled. If you are a risk-taker and dreamer with a desire to reach the world for Christ using evolving technology, then you will be inspired as you read *Multiplying Disciples.*"

—Nancy Wells, Heart-Cry for Revival Conference

Multiplying Disciples

Social Media and the *New Roman Road*

~

Sammy Tippit

An Imprint of Iron Stream Media
Birmingham, Alabama

Iron Stream Books
100 Missionary Ridge
Birmingham, AL 35242
An imprint of Iron Stream Media
IronStreamMedia.com

Library of Congress Cataloging-in-Publication Data.

Tippet, Sammy, author.
Multiplying disciples : social media and the New Roman road / Sammy Tippet.
Birmingham, Alabama : Iron Stream Books, an imprint of Iron Stream Media, 2020.
LCCN 2020021804 (print) | LCCN 2020021805 (ebook) | ISBN 9781563094064 | ISBN 9781596690622 (ebook)
Technology--Religious aspects--Christianity. | Social media--Religious aspects--Christianity. | Discipling (Christianity)
LCC BR115.T42 T565 2020 (print) | LCC BR115.T42 (ebook) | DDC 261.5/2--dc23

ISBN-13: 978-1-56309-406-4
Ebook ISBN: 978-1-59669-062-2

1 2 3 4 5—24 23 22 21 20

Dedicated to the followers of Jesus in Brazil, India, Iran, and Pakistan, who have taught me so much about multiplying disciples.

Contents

～

Acknowledgments

So many people have been instrumental in molding my thoughts about multiplying disciples and the great opportunity that has been afforded the church through social media. I mention many of them in this work. I truly appreciate their input.

I appreciate the input of my wife Tex. She has stood with me in this journey and has been a great encouragement as I've dreamed about things that seemed impossible.

I also want to thank the team at Iron Stream Media. Marty Lively has been a friend and prayer warrior as I have worked on this project. I appreciate Ramona Richards and Reagan Jackson for their thoroughness in the editing process. It has been such a joy to work with the entire Iron Stream Media team.

Foreword

~

Multiplying Disciples may be one of the most inspirational books you'll ever read, by one of the most indefatigable Christ followers I've ever known. Since I met Sammy Tippit nearly fifty years ago, I've been humbled—and often convicted—by his singular desire to win people for Christ. Obedient to his call to evangelize, he has preached in stadiums all over the world and shared his faith one-on-one, letting nothing stand in the way—meager resources, opposition, arrest, tragedy, grief, cancer, you name it.

Now, when many his age are winding down and passing the torch to a new generation, comes his most exciting effort yet to spread the good news of the Gospel of Jesus Christ. You'll be amazed at the power of this simple approach to maximizing social media to reach millions.

Because of the privilege of having written the Left Behind series, I am often asked if this or that bit of international news is evidence of Christ's imminent return. I'm neither theologian nor scholar and always hesitate to ascribe biblical portent to even earth-shattering events. But it doesn't take any deep insight to point to ultimate truth, uttered by Jesus Himself, when He told His disciples that "This gospel of the kingdom will be preached in all the world as a witness to all the nations, and then the end will come" (Matthew 24:14 NKJV).

Looking for signs of the coming of Jesus? Read *Multiplying Disciples* and you can do more than watch and wait. You can be part of the movement that brings it about.

Jerry B. Jenkins
Best-selling author

Innovation and Revival

It seems strange that I would ever consider writing a book about innovation. I consider myself a revivalist/evangelist, not an innovator. My heart passionately desires to reach the world for Christ, and my lifelong pursuit has been to fulfill the great commission that Jesus gave His followers—*go into the world and make disciples.* As I've traveled the path of world evangelization, I've discovered that the greatest evangelistic harvests in the history of the church have come during seasons of spiritual awakening—times of great outpourings of the Holy Spirit.

I came to know Christ during the Jesus Movement, a period in which the Holy Spirit moved across America transforming a generation of youth. During the 1980s and 1990s, God gave me the wonderful privilege of witnessing an historic movement of the Holy Spirit in Romania. An entire nation was delivered from the chains of atheism and communism. More recently, I've spent much time ministering among Iranians where perhaps the greatest outpouring of the Holy Spirit in Persian history is taking place.

But what do all of these great works of the Holy Spirit have to do with innovation? Or perhaps a more important question is, "What does innovation have to do with the outpouring of the Holy Spirit?" To be honest, I hadn't even considered these questions before the last couple of years. *However, I've come to believe that we're poised for the greatest move of God's Spirit that the church has ever known.* I know. That's a huge statement. But it's not unfounded. My assumptions are rooted in what I've witnessed in the last few years as well as on a study of biblical and historical precedents. The potential width, breadth, and depth of a mighty outpouring of God's Spirit are mind-boggling when we understand the biblical and historical connection between innovation and revival.

If you are a pastor, leader, or faithful member of a typical American church, you're probably scratching your head by now. And for good reason. Most of what we hear on news broadcasts tells us just the opposite. The struggles you see within your congregation speak even louder. Statistics about the state of the church flash warning signs that the church is flying headfirst into disaster. I'm a member of a church that is a part of the largest non-Catholic denomination in America, the Southern Baptist Convention (SBC). As I write this manuscript, there has been an historic decline in evangelism in the SBC. Baptisms from people coming to Christ have declined annually for seventeen years consecutively.

As these dire signals burn brightly in Western civilization, there's also an unprecedented spiritual harvest that's taking place around the world. Innovation plays a major role. Many of my American friends love gadgets and cool technology. But we don't view technological innovations in the same way that much of the rest of the Christian world sees them. They see them as tools given by God for the spreading of the gospel. A vast majority of Christians are using Facebook, Instagram, Twitter, and other social media sites, but they are primarily seen as a way to connect with friends and family or market what they are doing. Very few churches see these tools as outreach methods. They use them as ways to tell the world about themselves rather than Jesus, the One they serve.

I recently poured my heart out to a group of Christian leaders who also have a passion to proclaim Jesus. I told them much of what I'm about to share with you in this book. I said, "If just a handful of you would embrace what I'm about to tell you, I'm certain that it would result in hundreds of thousands of people coming to Christ, perhaps millions." I explained how revival and innovative technology had enabled me to see the greatest harvest that I've ever experienced. However, I didn't use the words *innovate* or *innovation* because I didn't view what I told them as some kind of innovation or even as being slightly innovative. I only saw what I had been doing as an attempt to solve a problem—reaching people with the good news of God's love during days of spiritual drought.

The group took a short break following my message. The next speaker addressed my presentation and said he thought innovation was a good thing, but it was not the answer to the circumstances facing our churches. He said prayer, repentance, and revival were the only things that could change our present situation. As I listened, I responded with both an "amen" and an "aha." *Amen* because I strongly believe we must have a great spiritual revival to change the climate in our churches. The first four books I wrote were about revival, repentance, and prayer. I agreed with everything the speaker said about renewal.

The Aha Moment

Then there was the aha moment. *Aha* because I finally understood the mentality that keeps us from experiencing such an awakening. It was a double aha because it was the first time anyone suggested I was being innovative in my approach. That caused me to look inwardly to see whether I was depending upon a clever innovation or upon God. I needed to ask some hard questions about the role of innovation and take time for some deep soul searching about its place in my ministry. After much reflection, I drew some definitive conclusions.

We've become experts in Western Christianity in creating spiritual dichotomies: holiness versus grace; the sovereignty of God versus the will of man; and evangelism versus discipleship. We've become adept at pitting great truths against one another and have lost sight of the beauty of the tapestry of God's Word. We've closed our eyes to see how the glory of God's holiness is intertwined with the splendor of God's grace. Holiness drives us to humility, and a humble heart becomes the soil in which grace grows our faith. When God's grace is applied, then our faith blossoms into holiness and makes us men and women of greater Christlike character. When we quit creating competing principles and start embracing contrasting biblical truths, we will be able to see the fullness and beauty of Christ in ways we never imagined.

Life-Changing Conclusions

After much prayer, study, and reflection upon what the speaker said, I realized that two sets of great biblical truths had been placed in competition with each other. Innovation and spiritual awakening aren't enemies. God has historically given us innovations so we can accomplish what He created us to do.

When the great truths of prayer, repentance, and revival are loaded on to the dock of innovation, the gospel can be transported to the most unreached peoples of the world. The gospel can spread beyond our wildest imaginations, even as it did in the first century.

What would you think if I were to tell you that your children and your grandchildren hold the keys to helping you reach thousands of people with the message of Christ? They've grown up with technology. It's second nature to them. They can help you. Would you believe me if I told you that without knowing anyone in Afghanistan, you could have 35,000 young people there listening to you teach the Bible every day? What would you think if I told you that with one extra staff member in your church, you could begin to disciple hundreds and perhaps thousands of people who speak Swahili in East Africa? Or what would you think if I were to tell you that you could begin to connect with people in your neighborhood who would never darken the doors of your church? Do you believe you could triple the number of people who listen to you teach the Bible weekly within the next year? If you are a Christian but not a leader in your church, do you think it is possible to turn your social media page into a ministry that could touch thousands of people around the world?

If the answer to any of those questions is yes or maybe, then I'm going to ask you to read the remainder of this book with an open heart, asking God to speak to you, send revival to your heart, and give you a fresh vision of what He wants to do in your life and church. And I can promise this—all of those things are within reach. How do I know? I've witnessed all of them happen in my own ministry and in the ministries of pastors and other Christians who have a passion for Christ and have embraced innovative ways to reach people with the message of God's love. I've seen how those who love the Lord can become instruments in God's hand by using the technology given this generation.

The greatest hindrance to the advancement of the kingdom of God lies within our thinking processes. I'm not talking about the power of positive thinking but rather the power of biblical thinking. It is when we meditate on biblical passages and bring our thinking processes captive to the obedience of those Scriptures that we experience revival. It's simply saying yes to God when He speaks to our hearts. It's aligning our thoughts with His thoughts. It's discovering the overriding truths of God's Word and acting upon them. I submit to you that the apostles Paul and Peter and the early church leaders did not view technological innovations as that which opposed the gospel but rather saw them as tools given their generation, which enabled them to obey the command of Jesus to preach the gospel to the whole world.

Definitions

Perhaps we need to pause for a moment and give definition to some of the terms I'm using. You don't have to agree with the definitions, but at least you will understand what I'm saying as we use them throughout the book.

Innovation is the introduction of something new, like an idea, method, or device. It is a novelty. Meanwhile, to *revive* means to return to life, as in to recover life or strength. It means to live anew, to become reanimated or reinvigorated. The original Greek word for revive, *anathalló*, means to thrive or flourish again. And *repent* means to turn from sin and dedicate yourself to amending your life. It is related to regret, contrition, and changing your mind. The original Greek word for repent, *metanoeó*, means to change one's mind or purpose.

Notice the common thread in those definitions—something new, a fresh change of heart and thinking, and a new direction and purpose. Repentance sets us free. Revival empowers us to move in God's direction. Innovation transports us where we need to go.

Our lives are like a sailboat that has been grounded by the storms of life. Repentance releases the grace of God to wash away the guilt that has created the mud that has bogged down our lives. The winds of revival then blow across our sails and move us into the sea of God's ultimate purpose. But innovation is our method of transport in which we travel across those waters. Every season of history demands a different means of transport. We must be cleansed before we can move in God's direction. We desperately need the empowering of the wind of God if we are to move into the world to make disciples. When we have the right boat at the right moment of history, there's no limit to where we can go. We can travel to the most distant parts of the world and proclaim the gospel to the most unreached peoples.

In the first chapter, I want to introduce you to three friends who have asked questions or made statements that have transformed my thinking about innovation and the outpouring of God's Spirit. They live on three separate continents, have different responsibilities, and have never met each other. However, they have impacted my life in such a powerful manner that it has resulted in millions hearing the gospel, many thousands coming to Christ, and hundreds of thousands of people being enrolled in small discipleship groups. One is a pastor in northern India, another a denominational leader in Brazil, and the third is the owner of a software development company in America. They are common, ordinary men who have used innovative methods to serve people and glorify Christ.

The people God uses are normally biblical dreamers. They think of ways to reach people for Christ and are always looking for a new means of transport for the gospel. They possess a similar mindset to Peter, Paul, and the early Christians. They don't think twice about using the technological advancements of their generation to preach and teach the Word of God. They are men and women full of the Holy Spirit, grounded in Scripture, and ready to board a ship to take them to dangerous places to proclaim the death, burial, and resurrection of Jesus. The color and model of the ship is of little importance to them. They just want to connect with the people at their destination. They don't see innovation as a competitor to the outpouring of God's Spirit. They believe that spiritual awakening and innovation usher in God's sovereign plan to fill the earth with people who know and love Him.

May 2020

Shortly after I submitted this manuscript to the publisher, an unseen enemy travelled to every inhabited continent, spreading death and destruction. This small virus was relentless in its devastation—killing hundreds of thousands, dumbfounding scientists, ravaging economies, and halting church services.

I've heard from Christian leaders around the world, telling me how difficult these days have been. At one point, more than half the world's population was in lockdown. The tragedies from COVID-19 have also hit close to home. I've lost friends to the deadly virus, and my heart breaks for their families.

It has been especially difficult for pastors and Christian leaders, as they have had to scramble to put together online worship services. The world changed overnight—and much of the church was not prepared.

However, my friends in Brazil, India, Pakistan, and I have observed a mighty move of God's Spirit during the darkness of 2020. I experienced the greatest evangelistic harvest of my life. We encountered God in the midst of the chaos.

During May 2019, my Brazilian friends and I dreamed of an evangelistic outreach that would be planted in the soil of discipleship during May 2020. We immediately began working on a strategy to reach one million people with the gospel and introduce them to small discipleship groups by utilizing social media and communication technology tools. We implemented many of the truths and methods presented in this book.

Friends from other countries joined and dreamed with us. We missed our target of one million people—but in a positive way. We shared the message of Christ with more than fifteen million people during May 2020! Hundreds of thousands of people prayed to receive Christ. Thousands of small discipleship groups were formed around the world. We multiplied disciples using social media in ways that went far beyond anything we could have imagined.

I invite you to dream, pray, and plan with us. You will learn in the following pages the biblical truths and strategies that we implemented, which resulted in disciples being multiplied around the world.

Chapter I

Dreams and Dreamers

Where there is no revelation [prophetic vision], the people cast off restraint; but happy is he who keeps the law. —Proverbs 29:18

The Bible provides several examples of dreams, visions, and interpreters of dreams and visions. They either impart knowledge about something in the future or point to God's will. For the purpose of this work, I am not describing the physical nature of a dream or vision but rather referring to the heart nature of dreams and visions—ones God places deep in the souls and minds of His leaders. God still imparts vision to His people, enabling them to look ahead and know how to accomplish His will.

Joel 2:28 (NIV) says, "And afterward, I will pour out my Spirit on all people. Your sons and daughters will prophesy, your old men will dream dreams, your young men will see visions." When our dreams flow from the heart of God, lives will be transformed, believers will grow in their faith, and God's kingdom will increase rapidly. The secret of a dream with a biblical foundation is the knowledge that our dreams are not self-induced but rather emanate from heaven.

I'm a natural dreamer, but some friends in Sicily have reminded me to always ask the question, "Is this a *good idea*, or is it a *God idea*?" Most of my ideas are good ones, but they are not necessarily ones birthed by God. I must test them to make sure they originated in heaven. *God ideas* will always be rooted in biblical truth. His Word does not change (Malachi 3:6). His promises are always *yes* and *amen* (2 Corinthians 1:20).

> *A dream that has been birthed by God will always place us on the path to obedience to the Word of God.*

God ideas always bring glory to Him and not to the dreamer. They place us on the path of God-exaltation, not self-adoration. They enable us to do what we were created to do—make disciples who will make disciples of the nations. They are rooted in humility and cause us to become more like Christ. They place us on a road called *walking by faith*. A dream birthed in heaven will always demand that we trust God. The fulfillment of the dream will extend beyond our reach, but not His. Paul wrote, "He who calls you is faithful, who also will do it" (1 Thessalonians 5:24).

There have been three men in recent years who have stimulated me to dream God's dream. Those dreams have produced innovative methods and resulted in an unprecedented harvest in my ministry.

The first person to impact me was Fabricio Freitas, a young pastor in Brazil. His parents encouraged him to read Christian books when he was a teenager. Two of my books, *Fire in Your Heart* and *The Prayer Factor,* had just been published in Brazil and were on the top of Fabricio's reading list. He developed a longing for spiritual awakening. I didn't know it, but God would use Fabricio to speak to my heart many years later.

I have ministered in Brazil since the mid-1980s, preaching at statewide and national conferences on spiritual awakening. When I turned sixty, God nudged my heart to add a new dimension to the ministry. He gave me a burden to meet with small groups of people in the countries where I travel and impart principles about revival and evangelism. The mandate was simple and direct: give rise to a new generation of evangelists who understand and practice the great truths of evangelism, which are rooted in revival.

The Good News in All the World
I started meeting with small groups of people with a burden and gift

to do evangelistic ministry. I soon met with twelve passionate Christian workers during one of my trips to Brazil. Pastor Fabricio Freitas was one who participated. By then, he had completed his education and was on staff at a prestigious church in Brasilia, the nation's capital. He soaked up truths about revival and evangelism and immediately put them into practice.

He implemented the revival/evangelism strategy with two hundred churches in the Brasilia area and saw great results. Many people came to Christ in most of the churches. His efforts were so successful that they caught the attention of the National Mission Board of the Brazilian Baptist Convention. They asked him to become director of evangelism for their denomination. Pastor Fabricio immediately contacted me and said, "We must teach these truths to all of our churches. Please come and help."

I set on a journey to mentor Pastor Fabricio. However, the opposite took place. He mentored me in so many ways. We conducted revival and evangelism conferences throughout Brazil. When I arrived in Brazil in October 2016, Pastor Fabricio accompanied me to several cities to speak. There was something different about our approach during this trip. It was a simple change but one that impacted me in a profound manner. It was so uncomplicated that I almost ignored it. I certainly didn't think it had much to do with revival or evangelism. For me, it was a cool, new tool, which was appealing to people his age.

Pastor Fabricio carried a small tripod to the places we traveled. When I stood to preach, he set up his tripod and connected it to his smartphone. He tapped a few icons as I walked on the platform. I then spoke to approximately two thousand attendees. God moved in hearts and lives. It was a wonderful time of seeing God transform people. After the service, Pastor Fabricio was even more animated when he said, "We had six thousand people who watched the meeting online, and we're getting very positive responses from them." *That's cool*, I thought. He gave a similar report every night and in every city.

I was intrigued enough to have Pastor Fabricio show me how to create a live Facebook message for my friends back in the United

States, and I gave them a one-minute update on our trip. More than eight hundred people viewed the video. However, the full impact of his reports didn't grab my heart and imagination until we returned to Brasilia. My interpreter, Dr. Alan Amorim, Pastor Fabricio, and I had breakfast at a hotel just before I returned to the United States. Dr. Amorim's father came to collect them at the hotel, and when he joined us for the meal, his voice trembled. "I watched you online as you spoke every night. God spoke deeply to my heart. As you concluded last night, I knelt in my home and prayed. God renewed my heart."

I was taken back. "Wow! That's wonderful!"

Dr. Amorim was excited to hear about his father's commitment to Christ. The young waiter pouring coffee into our cups was one of Dr. Amorim's students. The young man interrupted, "Yes, I listened every night, and God worked deeply in my heart also."

My heart leapt! My entire thinking processes changed in that moment. I heard everything that Pastor Fabricio had been telling me with a new filter. Six thousand people watching our services on Facebook was no longer a great statistic. This was no longer "virtual reality." These were *real* people with *real* life situations who made *real* commitments to Christ.

I had already begun doing some innovative online ministry in India, and my friend Pastor Jolly had been posting the videos on Facebook. I thought it must be very complicated, so I never attempted to film or post anything personally. Before I left Brasilia, I asked Pastor Fabricio, "Do you think I could do this?"

"I am certain you can, Pastor Sammy," he responded.

After I returned to the United States, I decided to make a short Christmas greeting from my wife and myself and publish it on my personal Facebook page. By the beginning of December 2016, I had more than two thousand Facebook friends and about eight hundred followers on our ministry page. Therefore, on December 2, I placed the greeting on my personal page. I discovered that the process was very simple. To my utter amazement, 9,200 people viewed the video, 361 "liked" it, and 159 people "shared" it. My mind spun as I watched people comment and share the video with others. One of the most important things that took place was that I began to dream. I saw the potential of reaching multitudes for Christ.

I knew I was sitting on something much bigger than anything I had ever attempted. One of the reasons the dream was so large was because of what had just transpired four days earlier in India. I'll share more about that in a moment.

I returned the next year to Brazil to speak at other revival and evangelism conferences. This time, Pastor Fabricio was no longer the one asking questions. He had already come up with a new technology tool that would multiply what we were doing. I asked everything I could think about technology and innovation. I needed to know more than just information about technology. I needed to think innovatively. That's when he said something that was a gamechanger. "Pastor Sammy, we are so grateful for the missionaries that came to Brazil more than one hundred years ago. They brought the message of salvation by grace through faith. They held evangelistic meetings that would last two or three weeks. God blessed their efforts. People came to Christ. Churches were birthed. Schools were started. Today there are millions of Evangelical Christians because of their efforts.

"When they came to Brazil, our country was a very rural nation. However, today, we are urbanized. The city of Sao Paulo has more than eleven million residents and greater Sao Paulo has more than twenty-one million inhabitants. By some other definitions of the city, it has twenty-seven million people living there and is the third-largest city in the world.

"Many people in Sao Paulo go to work early in the morning and don't get home until late in the evening. It's physically impossible for them to go to a three-week evangelistic meeting. We have been using the methods of these godly missionaries to reach Brazil today. We've used a nineteenth-century wagon to carry the gospel to a twenty-first century people, and we're being left behind. We cannot change the cargo. We *must not* change the cargo! It's precious! It's too valuable! But we must change the means of transportation!"

Pastor Fabricio's words pierced my heart and changed my perspective. The mentored became the mentor. But he wasn't the only young man to challenge my thought process.

New Transportation for Ancient Cargo

Pastor Jolly Sidhu in northwest India has made a substantial impact upon my thinking about innovation in ministry. Like Pastor Fabricio, he introduced me to a simple but powerful vehicle to transport the gospel to the most unreached peoples in the world. Jolly is not his real name but a nickname that he chose after he became a Christian. He grew up in a non-Christian home and had nothing to do with Christianity until he encountered a Christian teacher at his school. The professor had moved to northern India from the southern part of the country, which has a larger Christian population than the north. Pastor Jolly had been doing drugs and had lost all sense of purpose in life when he met the teacher. As a result of their relationship, Pastor Jolly came to Christ and became an ardent follower of Jesus.

An older pastor took Pastor Jolly under his wing and became a spiritual father to him. When I came to their state to conduct evangelistic events, the older pastor asked Pastor Jolly to interpret for me. He was so hungry to learn and grow in his faith. I spent hours after breakfast and lunch answering his questions.

He eventually planted a church in a city where very few Christians lived. I went to the church, which had about thirty-five people attending the services. I spent time teaching those new believers how to walk with Christ and share their faith. I trained Pastor Jolly in a similar way as Pastor Fabricio. I taught principles of prayer, revival, and evangelism. He translated the messages, and we filmed them in his language. Pastor Jolly was not only excited about the teachings, but he quickly put them into practice in his new church. The church grew rapidly. We occasionally talked via Skype video technology after I returned to the United States. One day in 2015 (about a year prior to my experience with Pastor Fabricio) he asked, "Sir, do you think you could disciple some of my leaders? Our church has grown so quickly, and we have so many young, new believers. They need discipleship. I think we could do it by Skype. I could attach my computer to a television screen, and they could see you. You could see them. I will translate. They could ask questions and interact with you. What do you think?"

"I don't know, Pastor Jolly, but we could try it. Do you have an internet connection that is fast enough?"

"We're on Skype right now. It will be as good as what we have now."

We decided to attempt it a few nights each week for three weeks. I would teach from my office or home, and they would gather at the church. The idea was so successful that Pastor Jolly then said, "I think we could have an evangelistic meeting doing this. What do you think?"

"I don't know. Let's try it."

A few weeks later Pastor Jolly connected his computer to a projector and sound system. I came into the meeting via Skype. I preached, and he translated. I saw the audience, and they saw me. I could see and hear them when they laughed. I paused and waited until they finished. I heard them when they shouted, "Amen." I gave a public invitation for them to become followers of Jesus. To our surprise, more than one hundred people prayed with me that night. Most of them became true followers of Jesus, were baptized, and are faithful members of Pastor Jolly's church today.

Pastor Jolly quickly followed up with me. "There was a man in the meeting who is a church planter. He wants to start a church in a village where there are no churches. He wants to know if we can do an evangelistic church-planting meeting in that village. What do you think?"

"I don't know, but we can attempt it." We did, and around one hundred people also came to Christ there. The church planter started a church with the new believers. We conducted four more evangelistic meetings during the year. They grew in numbers and response each time. Finally, Pastor Jolly said to me, "We need to think big. We need to dream of what God might do with this."

I asked him what he had in mind. "I'm thinking of a meeting with ten thousand people in attendance," he responded.

I chuckled. "Do you really think ten thousand people would gather in one place and want to listen to an American preach by video from his home in America?"

"I don't know, but I think we ought to try it."

We did. I was blown away! More than ten thousand people gathered on November 30, 2016, in a city in northwest India. We decided we needed to beef up our technology standards. We were able to obtain a stronger internet connection. I no longer just sat in my chair, but I stacked boxes in my office so I could have my laptop the same height as my face. I stood and preached. I gestured. I raised my voice. I lowered my voice. I could see the people. They tracked with me the entire message. I gave an appeal for people to become followers of Jesus. Thousands responded. They came to the platform where Pastor Jolly was translating. I prayed with them. Tears flowed. They cried out to the Lord. God moved mightily.

Pastor Jolly and I spoke the next day via Skype. We knew we needed to do something to help all these new believers. This conversation took place a month and a half after I had been with Pastor Fabricio in Brazil and watched him use his smartphone to broadcast our meetings live on Facebook. It was four days before I made my first video and placed it on my personal Facebook page. Pastor Jolly and I had already recorded some messages on revival and evangelism. We had also been working on an app for new believers. I had recorded some videos in English, and he had translated them into his language.

I told Pastor Jolly, "Let's start a Facebook page for the new believers. We already have a month's worth of videos ready for them. I could create videos in English, and you can translate them into your language. Let's encourage the new believers to go to the page. Let's create a Facebook page and begin posting them January 1, 2017."

We went to work immediately on translating short three-minute discipleship messages and posting them on my ministry page in English and on the Indian page in Pastor Jolly's language. I was shocked at what happened. We had more than five hundred thousand views that first month.

I posted the first video right before I ate breakfast. After eating I checked to see what had happened. I couldn't believe what I saw. More than one thousand people had watched the English video while I ate breakfast. Scores of people commented. Atheists, Muslims, Hindus, and Christians from around the world were watching and commenting. Many began sharing the videos. I contacted Pastor

Jolly and asked what was happening on his end. The same thing had taken place, but to an even greater extent.

We continued creating, translating, dubbing, and posting discipleship videos every day. By May 2017, we had one million views per month. I knew I had stumbled upon a very powerful boat to carry the most precious cargo in the world. I decided to build more boats. I already had translation teams in place for the discipleship app we were working to provide. I decided to use the translation work for the app to build more ships to sail on social media. By January 2019, we had eleven language pages on Facebook with an average of 6.5 million views every month.

The numbers of people watching the videos isn't what stunned me. It's where they were coming from that caused me to fall on my face and cry out to God in thanksgiving. The country where we have the largest following is Afghanistan with close to thirty thousand people who follow our Farsi (Persian) language Facebook page. Since the time that we began using Skype for evangelistic outreaches, we've planted several churches by using both Skype and Zoom technology. I've preached to as many as twenty-five thousand people in one setting, and we've begun more than one thousand small discipleship groups in India. We have grown in two years from two thousand friends on my personal page and eight hundred followers on my ministry page to nearly 150,000 followers of our ministry pages and five thousand friends on my personal page.

Both Pastor Fabricio and Pastor Jolly took a simple tool and immersed it in a big dream, which resulted in thousands of people coming to Christ and growing in their faith. I looked at a smartphone and saw a way to visit with friends. Pastor Fabricio looked at the same smartphone and saw a way to multiply the size of the audience who would hear the message about revival and evangelism. I used Skype as a way to connect with my friends in India. Pastor Jolly used it to disciple new believers in his church and to proclaim the gospel to thousands of people. Innovation accelerates revival when we begin to see technology through the lens of the great commission of Christ. When we dream God's dream, we embark upon a journey that will take us to places and people that we thought were impossible to reach.

First Steps

That's what Herman Spencer, the CEO and founder of Software Built by Design, taught me. When I first began looking at the possibility of using technology to transport the gospel, I met with Herman. He is a follower of Jesus who has a heart to provide education for people in nations who have limited access to education. He promised to help me develop technology tools to disciple new believers.

During our early discussions, I questioned Herman about what could or could not be done with technology. He smiled. "Sammy, if you can find something we can't do, then I will be forced to find a way to solve that problem. It will make my company a better one." Then Herman made a statement that changed my paradigm. He said, "You dream. Then you tell me what your dream is."

Wow! I had never thought in those terms. I asked myself, If I could do anything with technology that I wanted, what would I do? I reached deep into my soul and pulled out a biblical truth that I had learned many years earlier.

It was the concept of *discipleship/evangelism*. It was the foundation of what I had taught pastors Jolly and Fabricio. It was what Jesus commanded His disciples before He ascended to the Father. It was what Paul wrote to young Timothy in his second epistle. Make disciples who make disciples who make disciples. Preach the gospel in the power of the Holy Spirit. Teach those who come to Christ to follow Him and to do the same with others.

I had learned these great principles of *discipleship/evangelism* when I was a pastor of an American military community in Germany. Our church experienced revival, and the church exploded in growth. I met with twenty men every Thursday morning, and my wife met with twenty women every Wednesday at noon. We taught them how to grow in Christ, share the gospel, and help others to do the same. We multiplied disciples and saw the glory of the Lord in our congregation.

Now technology could enable me to cross borders and meet with people around the world at any time of the day or night. I would learn to win people to Christ while I slept and make disciples while I ate breakfast. A dream was birthed. A decision was made. I took my first step on the Roman Road.

Chapter 2

The Roman Road

~

To everything there is a season, a time for every purpose
under heaven. —Ecclesiastes 3:1

The timing of the arrival of Jesus to earth was no accident. Neither
were the other major events that occurred at that moment in human
history. Scripture tell us Jesus came in the fullness of time (Gala-
tians 4:4). His coming was on God's timetable to fulfill the proph-
ecies about the coming Messiah. God's people were longing for the
advent of the Christ. Two hundred years before Jesus arrived, God
had prepared historic technological and engineering feats to enable
the church to fulfill Christ's final command.

Be Fruitful and Multiply

In order to understand how incredible this moment was, we must
first grasp the original intent of God when creating man. The first
command He gave was to "be fruitful and multiply; fill the earth"
(Genesis 1:28). Man had not yet rebelled against God when the
instruction was given. God's desire was that the world be filled
with humans just like Adam—people created in His image, those
who walked in intimate fellowship with Him. God knew that the
only way humankind could do what He had created it to do was
to *choose* to love and obey Him. He didn't create humans as com-
puters that could only do what had been programmed. He created
humans as living souls, people with the ability to think, feel, and
choose.

A choice isn't truly a choice unless the person making the decision has the ability to make the wrong one. Man made the wrong choice. After making a decision to live outside of God's love and authority, humankind multiplied. But rather than multiplying the beauty of a loving relationship with God, evil multiplied, and darkness covered the planet.

God sent His judgment and started fresh with humankind. When Noah came off the ark, the first thing God told him was the same thing He told Adam—"Be fruitful and multiply, and fill the earth" (Genesis 9:1). God's intent had not changed, but we discover that Noah also made poor choices.

Then God looked upon Abram and found a man of faith. He told him, "I will make My covenant between Me and you, and will multiply you exceedingly" (Genesis 17:2). It's interesting that the same word *multiply* is used. One of the descendants of Abraham was Jesus, and the ultimate fulfillment of God's promise to Abraham came through Him. Jesus made the way for man to have that wonderful, loving relationship with God when He died on the Cross, taking the punishment for man's sin. He gave man the power to make the right decisions in life when He arose from the grave. He conquered man's worst enemies: sin, death, hell, and the grave.

Jesus then told His followers to go and "make disciples of all the nations" (Matthew 28:19). He also told them to baptize those new followers in the name of the Father, Son, and the Holy Spirit. But He added one more short statement that became critical for the fulfillment of God's original intent and His ultimate strategy for the church. He told the disciples to teach the new believers to do all He had commanded. What had He just commanded? Make disciples! Thus He instructed the disciples to make disciples who would make disciples who would make disciples. It's just another way of saying, "Be fruitful and multiply." The followers of Jesus had come into a right relationship with God through the death, burial, and resurrection of Jesus. They were now commissioned to bring others into this relationship and make them learners of Jesus who would do the same as they had done—in short, multiply spiritually.

Power From On High

However, these new followers of Jesus faced a great obstacle, which they could clearly see in the mirror. These people weren't world changers. The best among them were fishermen, tax collectors, cowards, and doubters. Yet it was said of them, "These who have turned the world upside down have come here too" (Acts 17:6). How could it be possible that such common people could change the world? They weren't great orators, scholars, or people of great wealth and influence.

Before ascending to heaven, Jesus had exhorted these simple men and women to "tarry in the city of Jerusalem until you are endued with power from on high" (Luke 24:49). They obeyed. They descended from the mountain to Jerusalem, and "these all continued with one accord in prayer and supplication" (Acts 1:14). The Holy Spirit came upon this ragtag band of men and women, and everything changed.

According to the Scripture, "They were all filled with the Holy Spirit and began to speak with other tongues, as the Spirit gave them utterance" (Acts 2:4). It really gets interesting from here. Jews from around the world were gathered in Jerusalem. They came from such faraway places that we know today as Iran, Turkey, Italy, Egypt, Arabia, and Libya. They all heard the disciples in their native language. The great miracle was not the disciples speaking in nonsensical tongues but rather that the people heard in their own languages. That has been one of the most powerful missionary principles since that time. Every person deserves to hear the gospel in his or her own language.

However, many Christians become obsessed with arguing about the implications of the disciples speaking in other tongues. Consequently, this disagreement often overshadows the beauty seen in the fulfillment of the original intent of God in the Book of Acts. There are parts of Acts that have received little to no attention. These bits of Scripture direct us to the Roman Road and the remarkable link between innovation, revival, evangelism, discipleship, and the original intent of God.

Perhaps there's one truth upon which we can all agree. These men and women could not have become world changers without the empowering of the Holy Spirit. It was in this great outpouring of God's Spirit that Peter the coward became Peter the courageous. It was what turned doubting Thomas into daring Thomas. It was what transformed the fishermen Peter, James, and John into fishers of men.

It's imperative to understand that all of the terrific technology, inspiring innovations, and super strategies are worthless without this empowering of the Holy Spirit in the life of the believer. Jesus told the disciples that the starting place to make disciples who will make disciples who will make disciples was the secret place of prayer. Spiritual multiplication really is spiritual! They needed to wait for the promise of the Father. They needed to be endowed with "power from on high" (Luke 24:49). The Roman Road would be useless without the deep work of the Holy Spirit in them and in those to whom they were to bring the wonderful gospel.

Revival is simply the manifestation of God's presence among God's people. When the Holy Spirit manifests Himself in the lives of His followers, a fire will be lit, and the world will rush to watch the flame of God's love burn in the church, and God's light will shatter the darkness. Lives will be changed, sins forgiven, and communities transformed. The word will be multiplied.

That's exactly what happened in the Book of Acts. Three thousand were "added" to the church on the day of Pentecost (Acts 2:41). Yet we find new terminology is used shortly thereafter. "The word of God spread, and the number of disciples multiplied greatly in Jerusalem" (Acts 6:7). A similar statement is made later. "But the word of God grew and multiplied" (Acts 12:24). The church moved from addition to multiplication and began to see the fulfillment of the original intent of God to multiply and fill the earth. Spiritual multiplication was a major factor in this historical account of the early church.

But what does innovation have to do with this great outpouring of the Holy Spirit? This is where we've neglected some simple observations in Scripture—those things that aren't very flashy but are absolutely necessary for the multiplying process and filling the earth with people who know and love Jesus.

Two cities in the Book of Acts were critical to the spread of the gospel: Jerusalem and Antioch. They became the hub of early Christianity. There's one characteristic that was common to both places: *prayer*. We find the leaders in Jerusalem waiting upon God (Acts 1:4, 12–14) and thousands are converted. We also find the leaders in Antioch praying and seeking God (Acts 13:1–5), and a great missionary movement is birthed. When we view what transpired in these cities through the lens of the original intent of God, we will be smitten with a sense of awe and wonder at the greatness of God. We will worship Him as we see the tapestry of His sovereignty in this moment of human history.

An oft-neglected question arises as we look at the outpouring of God's Spirit on the day of Pentecost. How did all those people from around the world get to Jerusalem? It was certainly a strategic crowd to start multiplying the good news of God's love. However, this didn't take place in the context of the twenty-first century where people hop on a plane and arrive at any destination in the world within twenty-four hours. This wasn't even the nineteenth century when the railway system was developed. This was nearly two thousand years before modern transportation. We often assume people from around the world were in Jerusalem and never ask how they arrived.

The Roman Road and the Fullness of Time

Two international road systems had been created approximately two hundred to three hundred years prior to the day of Pentecost. Ancient Roman engineers constructed the most remarkable system of travel the world had ever known. Military dominance of the empire was its primary purpose. Close to the same time of the construction of the Roman roads, the Silk Road was established. Its main design was for commercial reasons. Neither of the road systems was established to enable followers of Jesus to bring their message of repentance and forgiveness of sin to the world. However, both roads enabled disciples of Jesus to launch a movement that would transform history. Both roads would be filled with danger and temptation, but both roads allowed the apostles and early followers of Jesus to proclaim the gospel, make disciples, start churches, and send epistles to new believers. These roads enabled Christians to turn the world upside down.

The Roman roads and the Silk Road had a profound technological impact on first-century Christians. Those roads resemble in many ways what can happen with the internet in the twenty-first century. The Roman roads have been described as magnificent.

> Roman engineers were audacious in their plans to join one point to another in as straight a line as possible whatever the difficulties in geography and the costs in manpower. . . . The network of public Roman roads covered over 120,000 km, and it greatly assisted the free movement of armies, people, and goods across the empire. . . . To achieve the objective of constructing the shortest routes possible between two points (often not visible one to the other), all manner of engineering difficulties had to be overcome. Once extensive surveying was carried out to ensure the proposed route was actually straight and determine what various engineering methods were required, marshes had to be drained, forests cut through, creeks diverted, bedrock channeled, mountainsides cut into, rivers crossed with bridges, valleys traversed with viaducts, and tunnels built through mountains. Once all that was done, roads had to be leveled, reinforced with support walls or terracing and then, of course, maintained, which they were for over 800 years.[1]

Of course, those who created the Roman roads had no concern for the original intent of God. They created the system for *Pax Romana* (Roman Peace). The military controlled the roads to ensure that there would be no uprisings in the empire. Yet, in God's providence, the Roman roads allowed people throughout the empire and around the world to be in Jerusalem at that moment in which the mighty

---

[1] Mark Cartwright, "Roman Roads," Ancient History Encyclopedia, accessed December 31, 2019, https://www.ancient.eu/article/758/roman-roads/.

rushing wind of the Holy Spirit fell upon that small band of men and women who followed Jesus. It was in *the fullness of time*, the moment the church would be launched into the world to fulfill God's original plan for man.

This understanding has impacted me greatly. God has blessed me with an incredible board of directors in my ministry. They are a group of people who love God, love me, and long to see the fulfillment of the original intent of God. During one of our recent meetings, we discussed the nature of the multiplying church in the Book of Acts. We explored a few questions that I have pondered for a year following our discussion. Why were there thousands of people coming to Christ in the first twelve chapters of Acts, but we don't see the same thing after chapter twelve? Could the church not sustain such an outpouring? Did it need time to assimilate the new believers? Why don't we find the word *multiply* after Acts 12:24?

Antioch and Beyond

After pondering and praying over these questions for several months, the answer seemed obvious. I had walked right past it every time I read through the Book of Acts. What changed after chapter 12? Simple. Chapter 13. When Dr. Luke wrote Acts under the inspiration of the Holy Spirit, he wanted us to know that the purpose of the outpouring of the Holy Spirit was never to provide a holy happy hour for followers of Jesus. The focus was never to be on the wonderful and miraculous events taking place. It's as though he abruptly moves his camera from the great things transpiring in Jerusalem and makes a sharp turn toward Antioch, the second important city in his historical account. He then zooms in on one man passionate about fulfilling the original intent of God—Saul, who became known as Paul after a prayer meeting in Antioch.

Immediately after writing in Acts 12 that the word multiplied, Luke records an important prayer meeting that took place in Antioch, in which five key leaders attended. It's significant that four of the five were Jewish believers who grew up in Gentile lands.[2] When we understand the situation surrounding the prayer meeting

[2] Alexander MacLaren, "MacLaren's Expositions, Acts 13:1—Acts 13:13," Bible Hub, accessed January 14, 2020, https://biblehub.com/commentaries/acts/13-1.htm.

taking place in Antioch, we understand how their hearts must have been influenced by the cultural circumstances in which they found themselves.

Antioch was not only a part of the Roman roads system, but it also was on the Silk Road. It was filled with a diverse mixture of cultures, fashions, and languages. In fact, "Art, religion, philosophy, technology, language, science, architecture, and every other element of civilization was exchanged along these routes, carried with the commercial goods the merchants traded from country to country."[3] The Silk Road ended at Antioch, the final destination for caravans coming from the west, and the last stop for goods traveling to Rome.

H. V. Morton described in his book, *In the Steps of St. Paul*, what the apostle would have seen as he traveled to Antioch, which would have included "bands of jugglers and dancing girls on their way to Antioch—cohorts on the march, merchants from Baghdad and Damascus with their silks, spices, and perfumes, itinerant Greek philosophers, gladiators, men with caged beasts for the circus at Antioch, pagan priests begging their way with a god in a tent; and somewhere in that crowd, symbols of the old world and the new, a Roman senator traveling."

Paul would have been affected by what he saw in Antioch as he attended that prayer meeting. The Silk Road and the Roman roads not only made Antioch one of the most strategic commercial and military cities in the world, they gave Paul a vision for a lost world for which Jesus died. When you read the epistles of Paul, you get a glimpse into his heart and what he proclaimed after that prayer meeting. He tells the Roman believers that he is "not ashamed of the gospel" (Romans 1:16), and he testifies to the church at Corinth that the message of the Cross was "the power of God" (1 Corinthians 1:18).

It was in a prayer meeting in Antioch that the Holy Spirit moved in Paul's heart. It was the Holy Spirit who called Paul and Barnabas. He sent them. He used them to shake the empire for the glory of God. It was the work of the Holy Spirit that launched Paul into that

---

[3] Joshua J. Mark, "Silk Road," Ancient History Encyclopedia, May 1, 2018, https://www.ancient.eu/Silk_Road/.

first international missionary movement. It was the Roman roads that took them where they needed to go.

Paul wasn't afraid to travel the Roman roads. There's no indication he contemplated not bringing the gospel to the world because the Roman roads were filled with sinful activities. In fact, when we look at his travels, he told everyone everywhere the good news. Traveling the Roman roads was merely a way of life during his generation. He didn't spend time analyzing the pros and cons of the Roman and Silk roads. He simply saw them as a tool to accomplish what Jesus had commanded.

It's exactly the same heart vision of Pastor Jolly in India and Pastor Fabricio in Brazil. They have been compelled by the Holy Spirit to make disciples who make disciples. They found two twenty-first century roads called the *internet* and *social media* to transport them to people throughout India and Brazil. I know both of them well enough to know that prayer is foundational to what they are doing. Now the Holy Spirit has sent them to bring the gospel and make disciples of people whom they had only dreamed of reaching.

Chapter 3

Explosion at the Intersection of Innovation and God's Intent

And when they had prayed, the place where they were assembled together was shaken; and they were all filled with the Holy Spirit, and they spoke the word of God with boldness.
—Acts 4:31

Innovation creates a fresh way to introduce the good news of the death, burial, and resurrection of Jesus to the masses. *Prayer* prepares people to receive the gospel. It releases the Spirit of God to crawl into hurting hearts and draw them to the Savior. *Proclamation* then communicates the greatness of God's love. It shatters the shell encasing broken lives. When the three cross paths, an intangible explosion occurs, resulting in spiritual awakening. Any of the three stand alone as a powerful instrument in God's hands. However, when the three traverse at the intersection of God's intent and His eternal love, entire communities are transformed and nations shaken for God's glory.

Innovation

Innovations, which have been born in prayer, enable followers of Jesus to perceive impossible situations as great opportunities. A Christian identifies a need. That person cries out to God for a solution. A dream is birthed. The believer discovers a new way to meet the need. The message is proclaimed, and God's power transforms lives and communities.

It's important to note that innovation isn't always associated with new technology. Innovative thought goes far beyond technology. It enables the innovator to view problems with a new set of eyes. It creates new methods, ideas, and ways to solve a problem. One of the great difficulties the church has historically faced is that she often becomes attached to the method of God rather than the God of the method and His message. God never changes. Neither does His message. However, the world continually changes. We must never become married to the method, but we must also never forsake that ageless message and the eternal God who gave it. A changing world will demand innovation. But the heart remains the same—empty and in need of knowing God's purpose.

One of my first observations when I traveled into communist Eastern Europe during the 1970s and 1980s was the lack of innovation and creativity in those nations. For instance, most Romanian apartment buildings and houses were painted a dull gray. The vast majority of Romanians didn't have transportation. However, if a person had a vehicle, it was a Romanian Dacia, and probably a white one. There was only one television channel—the government station. The same was true throughout other Eastern bloc countries and especially in the former Soviet Union.

Life began to change in the Soviet Union under the leadership of Mikhail Gorbachev. Much of his leadership was marked by his *perestroika*, a reformation of the economic and political systems. In order to institute the reforms, more open government and broader circulation of information called *glasnost* was implemented. His new policy birthed a cataclysmic shift in the communist world.

When a believer's heart is set upon the original intent of God, that person views the changing world with a new set of eyes. The impossible suddenly becomes possible. The innovative Christian sees the hand of God in human history and cries out for an outpouring of His Spirit. Revival descends. Multitudes come to Christ.

Moments of historical change produce great opportunities for the gospel.

Vasile Binzar was such a person. During those days of momentous change, he worked with the youth of the Baptist church in Kishinev, the capital of the Moldovan Republic of the USSR. When he went on the streets, he saw open discussions and debate. He had never witnessed anything like it. He tested the waters by preaching the gospel outdoors, something that had never been done. Then something even more important transpired. He began to dream. He cried to God for revival among His people.

Not long after Vasile's experience on the streets and shortly prior to the first democratic elections in Romania, Dr. Titus Coltea, a Romanian friend, and I arrived in Kishinev. We met with Moldova's Christian leaders and told them of an amazing breakthrough in Romania. We had preached a historic evangelistic event in a stadium in northern Romania, and many people came to Christ. An innovative spirit captured the hearts of the Moldovan Christian leaders who heard our story. They dreamed that the impossible would take place in Soviet Moldova. The dream—an evangelistic event in the Stadium of the Republic.

I returned a few months later and preached that event. Thousands of people responded to the invitation and became followers of Jesus. The Moldovans then joined with the Romanians and a small band of Americans to travel to Ukraine to proclaim Christ there. Vasile Binzar, whose wife was from Ukrainian background, led the Moldovans. He dreamed of stadiums being filled. God answered his prayers, and multitudes came to Christ. An innovative spirit captured Vasile's heart. Vasile saw a problem that had plagued the church in the Soviet Union—churches had been forced to proclaim the message inside its four walls. Now Vasile dreamed of taking the gospel to the masses outside the church walls and into forbidden and dangerous places in the USSR.

God touched Vasile's heart after he read an article in a magazine about Norilsk, a city in the Siberian region of Russia. The city had a dark and chilling history. It's located in the Arctic Circle, and in 2017, *The New York Times* described its sordid past, "Built on the bones of slave prison laborers, Norilsk began as an outpost of Stalin's Gulag, a place so harsh that, according to one estimate, of 650,000 prisoners who were sent here between 1935 and 1956, around 250,000 died from cold, starvation or overwork."[1]

We had seen God transform lives in Romania, Moldova, and Ukraine. But was it possible to preach the gospel where Stalin murdered hundreds of thousands of people? Vasile, armed only with prayer and an idea, traveled to this dark and desolate city. An innovator always becomes a risk-taker. Vasile took the risk, traveled to Norilsk, and sought to find anyone who believed in God. If he could find someone, he would attempt to set up an event in the city to share the good news of the death, burial, and resurrection of Jesus.

Prayer Prepares Hearts

It's important to understand that innovation and superiority of speech will not transform lives. The conversion of the human heart is an eternal work of the Holy Spirit. Otherwise innovation becomes merely a cool idea, and proclamation is left to an elite group of orators and academicians. Prayer provides the fuel for the fire needed to burn in the heart of every follower of Jesus, and it opens the windows of heaven for the wind of God to blow across hearts and spread throughout churches, communities, and nations. Prayer teaches us that we can do all things through Christ (Philippians 4:13), and without Him we can do nothing (John 15:5).

Prayer was not only the launching pad for the early church but has played a major role in every great awakening throughout her history. Innovation took the movement of God's Spirit to new places and people, but we must never forget that the movement was in its essence a movement of *God's Spirit!* And prayer releases the Spirit of God to accomplish what is in the heart of God.

When Vasile arrived in Norilsk, he couldn't find any followers of Jesus. He prayed and asked God to lead him. Finally, someone told him there were a couple of "old ladies" who believed in God. He obtained the phone number of one of them and called. However, her husband answered, and he was drunk. He wouldn't allow Vasile to speak with his wife. After a few more attempts, he finally spoke with

---

[1] Andrew Higgins, "The Lure of a Better Life, Amid Cold and Darkness," *The New York Times*, December 3, 2017, https://www.nytimes.com/interactive/2017/12/03/world/europe/norilsk-arctic.html.

him when he was sober. The husband wanted to know why this Moldovan wanted to talk with his wife. After Vasile assured her husband that he had no interest other than talking with her about Jesus, the husband gave Vasile permission to speak with her.

When Vasile met the woman, she told him the most amazing story. This lady and her two friends had met together for years to pray. They asked God to work in the city but saw nothing happen. However, in 1988, *glasnost* was the order of the day, and at the same time, it was the one-thousandth anniversary of Christianity in Russia. They took a huge step of faith and approached the mayor of the city and asked for a building to conduct church services. To their surprise, the mayor agreed. Because of *glasnost* and the anniversary of Christianity in Russia, he told them the city would build a church for them. He sent them to the city architect with instructions for him to come up with a plan for a church.

The ladies went back to their apartments and wept, thanking God for answered prayer. It wasn't long before they became embarrassed and intimidated. The city's chief architect came up with a plan for a beautiful church that would hold a few hundred people. They had not told the mayor or the architect that there were only a handful of Christians in the city. What would happen when they found out that only a couple of "old ladies" would be attending?

The planning and the construction of the new church took a couple of years. Before it was completed, Vasile came to town with an innovative idea—conduct a mass evangelistic event in the city's stadium. The ladies and Vasile trembled when they discussed this new and innovative outreach. The prayers of two little "old ladies" had moved heaven to earth.

Proclamation of the Gospel

Our team continued to grow as we moved deeper into the heart of the Soviet Union. We now had Moldovans, Ukrainians, Romanians, and Americans working together to reach the most unreached area of the Soviet empire. Moldovan young people traveled to Norilsk to prepare for a great evangelistic event in the stadium. The grandparents of some of those Moldovan youth had died in Joseph Stalin's slave labor camps in Norilsk. Their grandkids were the first to take the gospel to the streets of that dark city. No one knew what to expect. Would a city built by slave labor (many of them Christians) and filled with atheists attend an outdoor Christian event?

I found the most horrible infestation of mosquitos when I arrived in Norilsk. I didn't see how I would be able to speak because they were so thick. Because the city is so far north, there's a very short birth season for them, and we arrived exactly at that moment. I couldn't open my mouth without mosquitos flying into it. It looked like disaster. However, there were two praying women in town. Nothing could stop their prayers, which meant that nothing would be able to keep me from preaching the gospel. An hour and a half prior to the start of the meeting, the winds blew, the rain fell, and the mosquitos disappeared.

A journalist interviewed me and asked, "Is our city under a curse? The streets upon which we walk were built by slave labor. The apartments in which we sleep and eat were built by slave labor. The offices in which we work were built by slave labor. Are we under a curse?"

I responded, "No. This city is not under a curse. It's under a blessing. Many of those who died building this city were Christians. I'm sure as they laid the pavement on the streets and the stones on the apartments, they prayed for the inhabitants of this city. You are under the blessing of their prayers. And today, you will be blessed by the good news of God's love found in Jesus."

Preaching in the stadium was one of the most remarkable moments of my life. It was a record attendance for any event in the stadium. After I proclaimed the life, death, burial, and resurrection of Jesus, I invited people to join me at the platform and pray. I was overwhelmed with the response as hundreds of people placed their faith in Jesus.

The new church building had just been completed a few weeks prior to my arrival. When I preached the following Sunday in the church, it was packed and overflowing. A spiritual explosion had erupted. Several young people who came to Christ in that meeting later went to Bible College in Romania. They are now ministering in Siberia and throughout Eastern Europe.

This has been the historic pattern of the church. Innovation causes us to evaluate a situation differently. Prayer forces us to look up. Proclamation makes us reach out to a needy world around us.

When innovation meets prayer and proclamation at the corner of God's intent and His love, revival erupts.

Look at Peter in Jerusalem. Hear Paul in Athens. Study Martin Luther in Germany. Walk with George Whitefield in America. What did they all have in common? They preached Jesus: His death, burial, and resurrection. The message never changed. It was a simple message, directed straight at the hearts of the hearers. They embraced what Paul wrote to the church at Corinth: "The message of the cross is foolishness to those who are perishing, but to us who are being saved it is the power of God. . . . For since, in the wisdom of God, the world through wisdom did not know God, it pleased God through the foolishness of the message preached to save those who believe" (1 Corinthians 1:18, 21).

Revivalists often espouse that renewal only comes when we pray. But prayer without the power of God through the message of the death, burial, and resurrection becomes benign because it bypasses the ultimate intent of God. Prayer without proclamation of the gospel is like having an accelerant but no wood for a fire. Powerful praying takes place when we pray according to the heart of God. We know what is on the heart of God because Scripture tells us, "The Lord is not slack concerning His promise, as some count slackness, but is longsuffering toward us, not willing that any should perish but that all should come to repentance" (2 Peter 3:9). God's longing is that all people turn from sin and trust in Jesus. When we pray according to His will and act accordingly, we place ourselves in a position to see a great move of God's Spirit.

Chapter 4

Historical Awakenings and Innovation

~~~~~

So, being sent out by the Holy Spirit, they went down to Seleucia, and from there they sailed to Cyprus. —Acts 13:4

Paul often traveled by ship to various parts of the Roman Empire. Throughout the Book of Acts he can be found sailing from such places as Seleucia, Philippi, Troas, Mitylene, Trogyllium, and numerous other communities. We can read over those passages without realizing how one innovation played a critical role in transforming the spiritual culture of the Roman Empire: the lateen sail. Until the second century BC, sailing was limited to ancient square sails, which could only be pushed along in the direction of the wind.

The Encyclopedia Britannica explains the importance of the lateen sail. "The lateen is believed to have been used in the eastern Mediterranean as early as the second century CE, possibly imported from Egypt or the Persian Gulf. Its effective use by the Arabs caused its rapid spread throughout the Mediterranean, contributing significantly to the resurgence of medieval commerce. Combined with the square sail, it produced the ocean-conquering full-rigged ship."[1]

The lateen sail changed the history of commerce, but the disciples used it to transform the lives of the citizens of the Roman Empire. Not long before Jesus commanded His disciples, "That repentance and remission of sins should be preached in His name to all nations,

---

[1] Editors of the Encyclopaedia Britannica, "Lateen Sail," Encyclopaedia Britannica, accessed January 14, 2020, https://www.britannica.com/technology/lateen-sail.

beginning at Jerusalem" (Luke 24:47), God prepared seagoing transportation to carry the early followers of Jesus across the Mediterranean and Indian Oceans. This innovative technology allowed Paul, Peter, Thomas, John Mark, and other early Christians the ability to bring the good news of God's plan of redemption around the world. The world had changed, and they seized the moment to fulfill the original intent of God. When the gospel, which had been undergirded by a powerful prayer movement, intersected with technological advancements, a spiritual awakening erupted and reshaped the Roman Empire.

The Reformation and Innovation

Perhaps the Reformation stands as the most glaring example of the move of God's Spirit through innovation. The advent of Johannes Gutenberg's printing press paved the way for the transformation of the church in Germany and throughout Europe. However, Gutenberg didn't invent printing. The Chinese had done that nearly a thousand years earlier, but their process was cumbersome, and the method didn't enable printing for the masses. Gutenberg's press gave the ability for mass printing.

Yet the Reformation still didn't take place when Gutenberg printed the Bible in 1455. His press initially created a sense of excitement throughout the continent because of the potential of the technology. But the business model for printing didn't fit the times, and Gutenberg went bankrupt. His life can best be described as *boom, bust, and pick up the pieces.* He struggled most of the remainder of his life. Sixty years after the first Bible was printed, an innovative monk with a passion for Scripture would be God's instrument to initiate the Reformation. Martin Luther used Gutenberg's technology to present the truth of the Word of God in a manner in which the masses could understand it.

Before Luther's ninety-five theses were nailed to the door of All Saints Church in Wittenberg, the printing press primarily provided literature to the educated class. When Luther published his theses, he realized that he could use Gutenberg's technology for the glory of God. Just as the apostles spread the gospel by using the lateen sail, Luther used the printing press to spread the Word of God.

Luther's theses were translated and published in German, the language of the people. Prior to his ninety-five theses, most publishing had been done in Latin. The common person didn't have the ability to read what had been printed. Luther lit a fire in the hearts of the German people when the common man was finally able to read the great biblical truths for himself. The Holy Spirit had caused people from around the world to hear the early apostles speak in their mother tongues. Now the German people could read the Scriptures in their own language. The power of God's Word in the language of the common people transformed the nation and set hearts aflame with the truths of God's word.

Luther preached clearly and concisely the Word of God. His ninety-five theses didn't produce a long book. They were the equivalent of an eight-page booklet filled with Scripture, text, and images. Because he presented the truths in a concise manner, the publishers were able to distribute them widely. He found an innovative way to overcome the greatest hindrance to book distribution—bulkiness. Martin Luther saw the potential of one technology, thought innovatively about how to use it for God's original intent, and then shook northern Europe and changed history.

Innovation of Outdoor Preaching in Early America

George Whitefield is considered among historians to be one of the most influential persons in Colonial American history. After hearing George Whitefield preach, Benjamin Franklin opined about the depth and breadth of his work, "It was wonderful to see the change soon made in the manners of our inhabitants. From being thoughtless or indifferent about religion, it seem'd as if all the world were growing religious, so that one could not walk thro' the town in an evening without hearing psalms sung in different families of every street. . . . Mr. Whitefield, in leaving us, went preaching all the way thro' the Colonies to Georgia."[2]

Field preaching was unheard of in eighteenth-century England as preaching was confined to indoor facilities. However, Howell Harris, a young Welsh evangelist who had a passion to reach people with

---

[2] Benjamin Franklin, *Autobiography of Ben Franklin* (Philadelphia: J. B. Lippincott & Co., 1869), 253–254.

the gospel, began preaching outdoors with great success, bypassing the elite and bringing the message of Christ to the masses. Any violation of the religious methods of the day unleashed the wrath of religious leaders. Although Harris became controversial, Whitefield sensed a kindred spirit when they met.

After Whitefield's encounter with Harris, he finally bit the bullet and stepped out in faith and preached outdoors, speaking to about two hundred people. He wrote in his journal, "Blessed be God that the ice is now broke, and I have now taken the field! Some may censure me. But is there not a cause?"[3] Whitefield's audiences quickly grew from two hundred to more than twenty thousand.

Whitefield's outdoor preaching shocked England and awakened the colonies. He learned a new method of preaching and perfected it. John Wesley followed his example and also started preaching in open fields. One of the great British preachers of all times, Charles Haddon Spurgeon, wrote, "It was a brave day for England when Whitefield began field preaching."[4]

Whitefield, Harris, and Wesley became known as *Methodists* because they employed innovative methods in their preaching. Passion for those in need of Christ, holiness of life, and courage to act on God-given innovations startled a generation and awakened the churches. Whitefield crossed the Atlantic thirteen times to preach in the colonies. The Spirit of God fell, and a nation was birthed.

The Necessity of Innovation and the Second Great Awakening

Charles Finney, an evangelist during the Second Great Awakening in America, became controversial among Christian leaders to a great extent because of the innovative methods he used to proclaim the gospel during the 1800s. Dr. Frank Harber, a scholar on Christian evangelists and evangelism, wrote about Finney and the Second Great Awakening, "Finney was often misunderstood because of his

---

[3] Ibid., 67.

[4] Charles Haddon Spurgeon, *Lectures to my Students: Being Addresses Delivered to the Students of the Pastors' College, Metropolitan Tabernacle*, 2nd series (London: Passmore and Alabaster, Paternoster Building, 1877), 66.

innovative methods. Finney believed that true revival and reformation never comes outside of new measures."[5]

Finney stated, "If we examine the history of the church we shall find that there never has been an extensive reformation except by new measures. . . . When [God] has found that a certain mode has lost its influence by having become a form, he brings up some new measure, which will *break in* on their lazy habits, and *wake up* a slumbering church."[6]

It was the Second Great Awakening that brought unity to the American people and gave them the courage and character to overcome what had the potential to destroy the new experiment of the young democracy. The roots of this spiritual revival took place in the most unlikely place—a cane field in rural Kentucky. A Presbyterian church had experienced a move of God's Spirit in one of the most crime-ridden areas of the new frontier. Word about the move of God's Spirit spread rapidly, and an estimated 25,000 gathered in those fields. The wind of the Spirit blew across the hearts of the people, transforming the culture and character of the nation.

I've visited that historic site and was amazed at some of the things I learned. Several truths captured my heart when I arrived in that field in rural Kentucky. It was the first truly American revival. The First Great Awakening took place because of great men and women who had come from Britain. But this work of God was a genuine American experience. Americans will never understand Evangelicals until they understand what happened in the Cane Ridge Revival.

New attitudes and a new measure emerged during the revival. It was egalitarian. This was a time when people were categorized by their race and economic status. However, whites, blacks, Native Americans, free persons, and slaves all worshipped together. A spirit of brotherhood filled their hearts.

It transformed cultural norms. Although many of the Christians in the South held to slavery, the Second Great Awakening produced

---

[5] Dr. Frank Harber, "An Examination of the Historical Development of the Ministry of the Evangelist within the Christian Church" (dissertation, Southwestern Baptist Theological Seminary, 1994), 118.

[6] Charles Finney, *Lectures on Revival of Religion*, 2nd ed. (New York: Leavitt, Lord and Co., 1835), 249.

a number of abolitionists, including Charles Finney. The leaders of the Cane Ridge Revival came under conviction about slavery and freed their slaves.

These old-time gospel camp meetings were the new method at the time to reach the people in the emerging pioneer culture. Testimonies abounded about the hardest and meanest of people being transformed by God's power when they placed their faith in Jesus at the camp meetings.

Innovation Today

As America progressed, the social and moral climate changed, and new methods were required to take the old biblical message of the gospel to the masses. God raised up Billy Graham, an evangelist from the hills of North Carolina, to take the gospel to more people than any other person in history. He wasn't the first to use television to proclaim the gospel to the masses; however, he used it in innovative ways. In 1995, Graham preached during a televised event that is considered the largest one-time Christian outreach in history. It is estimated to have reached a global audience of one billion people and was interpreted into 116 languages in 185 countries. He used satellite television to launch one of the most innovative methods of proclaiming the gospel in the history of the church.

This televised event inspired other evangelists to think and act innovatively. The Graham outreach not only obtained historic proportions, but it also opened the way for the largest evangelistic outreach in modern Egyptian history. Evangelist Luis Palau was asked in 1998 to preach in Egypt's largest Evangelical church. The church built upon what had been done with Billy Graham a few years earlier and filmed Palau nightly from March 12–15. Couriers then took VHS videos to 569 church locations throughout the country.

Because the Graham and Palau outreaches were so successful, the church and the Egyptian network asked me to preach a similar meeting in 2000. The outreach went beyond everyone's expectations. This time, more than 600 churches throughout Egypt participated. The crowds exceeded 150,000 per night, and thousands placed their faith in Christ. Everyone who followed Jesus was brought into a small discipleship group within seventy-two hours.

My eyes were opened in Egypt to the incredible possibilities of reaching the world by using technology in innovative ways. What I witnessed stirred my soul and enlarged my vision to see the fulfillment of God's original intent. It caused me to seek Him for the greatest Christian revival in history. At one point in my ministry, I became intimidated by the opportunities afforded us to reach the world with the gospel. A friend encouraged me, "The way you go forward is by remembering what God has done in the past."

When I look back at the great outpourings of God's Spirit, I see innovators wrestling in prayer, pursuing holiness of life, depending upon the Holy Spirit, and proclaiming the good news of Jesus. There's never been a time in history when the church has had the opportunities that we have today.

We move forward by looking back at the great moves of God's Spirit. We learn. We pray. We dream. We surrender. We believe. We proclaim. We disciple. And soon He comes!

Chapter 5

Dangers and Temptations

~~~~~~

From the Jews five times I received forty stripes minus one. Three times I was beaten with rods; once I was stoned; three times I was shipwrecked; a night and a day I have been in the deep; in journeys often, in perils of waters, in perils of robbers, in perils of my own countrymen, in perils of the Gentiles, in perils in the city, in perils in the wilderness, in perils in the sea, in perils among false brethren; in weariness and toil, in sleeplessness often, in hunger and thirst, in fastings often, in cold and nakedness—besides the other things, what comes upon me daily: my deep concern for all the churches.
—2 Corinthians 11:24–28

I couldn't believe what I was reading. A friend in Iran sent an email expressing his amazement at what he had just seen. He said one of the leading universities in Iran had published my testimony on the home page of their website. His email included a link to that page.

Iranian friends had previously translated our ministry's website into the Persian language, and it included the account of how I came to Christ. The Iranian University had evidently seen and copied my testimony from our ministry's Persian website and posted it on their own home page.

I immediately contacted an Iranian American friend and asked her to check it out, as I cannot read Persian. She was even more amazed. She said the university's page not only contained my story, but they had also not changed anything from the testimony they took from my ministry's Persian webpage, including an invitation for people to become followers of Jesus.

I wondered how this could have happened. To this day, I don't know. I also thought, *a very brave person is going to be in huge trouble.* What I didn't realize was that I was the person about to have problems. Within a few weeks, I had my first encounter with what I call *spiritual cyber warfare.*

Someone from an unknown location gained access to the Sammy Tippit Ministry's server and hacked our language websites. The hacker deleted all of our language sites. Those sites contained discipleship devotions that helped new followers of Jesus to grow in their faith. Because we ran our English site on a different server, it went untouched. The hackers were savvy in the manner in which they destroyed the sites. A few seconds prior to attacking the sites, they deleted everything on the backup server. They destroyed our websites, our backup websites, and all our translated information. It was discouraging to say the least. We had to recreate new websites for all our languages, which cost much time and money.

Many Christians are skeptical about using innovative technology because of incidents like this. That's understandable. However, we must allow the Holy Spirit to fill our hearts, cast out all our fears, and fill us with His love. If our ministry would have done nothing else after the attack, then there were still thousands of Persians who had heard what Christ does in a person's life. However, we recreated the websites and now have even more technological outreaches. Why? Because God loves people. Persian people. All people. When we're consumed with the love of God, we will love like He loves. Nothing can stop us from fulfilling His original intent. Our hearts will be filled with love for Him, for others, and we will refuse to give up.

The Apostle Paul's Dangers and Difficulties

Paul could have easily quit. He faced difficulties shortly after he began his first missionary journey. Jews opposed him. Romans imprisoned him. False apostles lied about him. Yet he remained faithful until death. What motivated the apostle? After listing all the difficulties, he clearly states the reason: "My deep concern for all the churches."

When Paul wrote to the church at Corinth, he not only listed the difficulties he faced from those who opposed the gospel, but he also detailed his plights that resulted from using the technology of the times: 1) forty stripes minus one, 2) beaten with rods, 3) stoned, 4) in perils of my own countrymen, 5) in perils of the Gentiles, 6) in perils in the city, 7) and perils among false brethren.

Paul also writes about the troubles he faced because he used the Roman roads and the lateen sail to bring the gospel to the nations. That list of tribulations appears to be longer than his record of problems he faced from opposition: 1) three times I was shipwrecked, 2) a night and a day I have been in the deep; 3) in journeys often, 4) in perils of waters, 5) in perils of robbers, 6) in perils in the wilderness, 7) in perils in the sea, 8) in weariness and toil, 9) in sleeplessness often, 10) in hunger and thirst, 11) in cold and nakedness.

The final four of the second list could possibly be attributed to his opposition, but they definitely resulted from his use of the technology of the times. There's one simple conclusion we can draw from Paul's experience—*innovative Christians who are committed to fulfill the original intent of God can expect problems.* All innovators face a multitude of challenges. A Christian innovator with a passion to reach the world for Jesus must be prepared to face both opposition and difficulties from traveling the modern Roman roads. Yes, there will be technical difficulties. Yes, there will be opposition. But there will also be the possibility of a great outpouring of God's Spirit and an unprecedented harvest.

When I first created Facebook pages in Punjabi and English, I was amazed at the number of views and the growth of young people watching the videos. As I mentioned in chapter 1, the number of views the first month blew me away: five hundred thousand. That number grew every month until we had one million views six months later. I knew I had tapped into something that could impact tens of thousands of people around the world. I recruited translation teams to create the discipleship/devotional videos in other languages. My goal was to add five more languages on my birthday, July 27, 2017. I thought it would be a blessing to begin to disciple people in seven languages on my seventieth birthday. We launched the other languages, and to my utter amazement, it went far better than I could have ever anticipated. Two of those languages, Persian and Hindi, grew to contain the largest following of any of our Facebook pages.

Death Threats and Disciples

There were a couple of interesting things that took place during and after the launch of those pages. Ninety-five percent of the people who became followers of those pages were under the age of forty-five. Yet I received more death threats on my seventieth birthday than in my entire life. The threats came from people my age, mostly living in Afghanistan. Yet it wasn't just old religious guys who tried to over-run our Facebook pages. Atheists and cult groups attempted to steal viewership.

One group who doesn't believe in the deity of Jesus started a hashtag movement called, "Sammy Tippit is a false preacher." What an honor! And what a blessing! One day, I followed the hashtag, only to discover that there was a trove of video messages by me. They all spoke about the deity of Jesus. Anyone following the hashtag could listen to scores of messages explaining Christ's divine nature.

The gospel will always produce opposition. Conflict shouldn't be a surprise.

Paul wrote to young Timothy, "Yes, and all who desire to live godly in Christ Jesus will suffer persecution" (2 Timothy 3:12). Anyone who wants to grow into the image of Jesus must anticipate adversity. It's a part of the package that comes with following Jesus. He reminded His disciples, "Remember the word that I said to you, 'A servant is not greater than his master.' If they persecuted Me, they will also persecute you. If they kept My word, they will keep yours also" (John 15:20).

Yet Paul's dangers and difficulties of taking the gospel to the non-Jewish world didn't just emanate from those who opposed the gospel. They also flowed out of the culture that emerged from the new technology. As the Roman roads developed, people with impure motives discovered how to exploit the system.

Dangers on Today's Roman Roads

The Roman roads had rest stations similar to the rest stops on our highways. These places served drinks, and some even served food. They were normally located sixteen to twenty miles from each other, and they often became a hangout for thieves and prostitutes. Danger and temptation lurked all along the path Paul traveled. He understood well the difficulties he faced as he traveled to fulfill God's original intent. Perhaps that was one reason he became so upset when his travel companions forsook him.

The internet and social media have provided incredible opportunities to proclaim the gospel and help people grow in their faith. However, we must understand and prepare for the tremendous temptations and dangers confronting anyone traveling today's Roman roads. Digital thieves lurk around every corner, and pornography can pop up unexpectedly. I know people who have had their entire bank accounts emptied because they fell for a well-crafted scheme to steal their possessions. I've seen families shattered because someone simply clicked a link that led the person into a dark pit of pornography. People with gambling or sexual addictions may need to refrain from traveling the modern Roman roads until they have found a consistent level of victory or created a system of protection from evil schemes along the road.

Numerous pitfalls await anyone traveling today's Roman roads. This generation of cyber thieves could not care less about the spiritual background of their victims. They'll take advantage of Christians and non-Christians alike. They often hide in the "dark web" and attack the weakest travelers at their most vulnerable moments. They search for those with naive minds and addictive habits. When they find them, they slither into their hearts and spew their deceptive venom. They will steal their money, reputation, and future. Christians who travel today's Roman roads must understand the dangers, prepare for the journey, and build spiritual cyber walls to protect them on the journey.

I'll not attempt to enumerate all the possible temptations and dangers we might encounter on today's Roman roads. There are enough temptations to fill an entire book with their descriptions, and it would be outdated in less than a year. However, there are three age-old temptations that have seduced every generation. They thrived on the ancient Roman roads and have multiplied exponentially on the modern Roman roads. The Apostle John identified them in his first letter. He wrote, "For all that is in the world—the lust of the flesh, the lust of the eyes, and the pride of life—is not of the Father but is of the world" (1 John 2:16). A quick way of stating John's observation is that "sex, silver, and self" are the great temptations seducing every Christian on his or her journey.

The following is a list of a few of the dangers facing the traveler on today's Roman roads.

The Lust of the Flesh (Sex)

I recommend that Christians utilize cyber barriers and accountability tools to monitor computer use on the internet. Following are some dangers and some excellent tools that will help individuals and organizations with concerns for themselves or those they love.

1. Sexual Predators—Parents need to talk to their children about the dangers of sexual predators who exploit children online. These predators comb the internet looking for vulnerable children and youth. Children between the ages of ten and seventeen are the most targeted age group by online predators. In fact, one in seven young people experience unwanted sexual solicitations online and one in three are exposed to unwanted sexual material online.

   Parents need to educate themselves and their children about the dangers online. I have found the Texas Attorney General's office provides some excellent resources to help parents work to protect their children at the following website: www.texasattorneygeneral.gov/initiatives/cyber-safety.

2. Pornography—The porn industry has flooded the internet and destroyed countless families. Webroot, a cyber security firm, presented some staggering statistics about the toll internet pornography has taken on our lives. It reported that it costs US business productivity that results in 16.9 billion dollars lost annually. Their report states that every second there

are 28,258 people watching pornography online and that $3,075.64 is being spent on it every second. Every day there are 2.5 billion emails sent or received that contain porn.[1]

The Lust of the Eyes (Silver)

Anywhere money is housed, thieves lurk in the shadows to break in and steal it. The Apostle Paul wrote about one of the great temptations of people throughout all generations, "The love of money is a root of all kinds of evil" (1 Timothy 6:10). The internet has opened the door to those with the love of money to destroy lives and empty bank accounts. Thieves no longer need a gun or knife to rob the vulnerable. Their weapon of choice has become a computer or smartphone, and their modus operandi is to attack the least protected.

1. Scams—Elderly persons on fixed incomes are often the most vulnerable. I know one lady who had her entire life's savings emptied by cunning cyber thieves. They convinced her she had won a million dollars but that she needed to pay the taxes on the money before she could receive it. She fell for the scam, and it wiped out her bank account and wreaked havoc on her future. It wasn't social media that they used. It was a simple smartphone and a slick-talking thief.

    The statistics alone are incredible. Bromium, a cyber security firm, reported cybercrime annual revenues worldwide are 1.5 trillion dollars. That figure includes:

    - $860 billion in illicit/illegal online markets
    - $500 billion in theft of trade secrets
    - $160 billion in data trading
    - $1.6 billion in crimeware-as-a-service
    - $1 billion in ransomware[2]

[1] "Internet Pornography by the Numbers: A Significant Threat to Society," Webroot, accessed January 15, 2020, https://www.webroot.com/us/en/resources/tips-articles/internet-pornography-by-the-numbers.

[2] Bromium, "Hyper-Connected Web of Profit Emerges, As Global Cybercriminal Revenues Hit $1.5 Trillion Annually," April 20, 2018, https://www.bromium.com/press-release/hyper-connected-web-of-profit-emerges-as-global-cybercriminal-revenues-hit-1-5-trillion-annually/.

I recommend that all readers check out the US government website, www.usa.gov/online-safety, that provides tips on keeping yourself safe and secure online.

2. Phishing Scam—Phishing is when a person disguises themselves as a trustworthy entity and attempts to receive sensitive information through online communication. This information may include usernames, passwords, or credit card information. These scams are normally carried out by email or text messaging, and they send the person to a genuine-looking but fake website where the individual provides personal information for the scammers.

Remember, legitimate companies won't ask you to divulge sensitive information online. If there is ever any question, I always go directly to the company that is "contacting" me to find answers. I don't ever answer a suspicious email and recommend that everyone find a savvy technical friend to talk to before responding to any suspicious text messages or emails.[3]

Pride of Life (Self)

Social media can easily create the opportunities to develop a narcissistic lifestyle. The greatest danger lurking in the dark corners of all of our hearts is that of pride. As I have watched the downfall of numerous Christian leaders over decades, it has been obvious that most of the downward trajectory began with pride. Pride resides in the dark closets of our hearts and can only be exposed by the light of the Holy Spirit.

A simple question needs to be asked about all of our online activity: Does my post bring glory to Christ? One of the reasons God uses technology in many areas of the world is because Christians view it as a way to glorify Christ rather than promote themselves. It would be interesting to know how many Christian websites promote their Christian organizations and ministries rather than reaching out to a hurting world. We will one day stand before Christ and give an

---

[3] Consumer Reports has an excellent article on how to protect yourself against online phishing scams at https://www.consumerreports.org/money/how-to-protect-yourself-from-phishing/.

account of how we used today's Roman roads. It will be a day filled with shame or joy. The choice is ours right now.

Perhaps the greatest danger that we face is that we don't see the modern Roman roads as God's gift to this generation. It's inevitable that we travel today's Roman roads. There's no way to avoid it. However, the looming question is, "What did we do when we traveled on them?" Did we glorify Christ, or did we simply join the millions of others who became consumers and self-promoters?

Faith or Fear?

We will always face dangers when we attempt to do God's will. The Scripture warns us, "Be sober, be vigilant; because your adversary the devil walks about like a roaring lion, seeking whom he may devour" (1 Peter 5:8). However, we must answer a critical question as we travel the new Roman road. Will we live by fear or faith? We must focus on Jesus, act wisely, and walk humbly. If we act accordingly, we will be "more than conquerors" on today's Roman road.

Chapter 6

Biblical Principles for Innovative Technology

For our gospel did not come to you in word only, but also in power, and in the Holy Spirit and in much assurance, as you know what kind of men we were among you for your sake.
—1 Thessalonians 1:5

People often ask how I am so successful in using social media to reach people with the gospel. They want a secret strategy, or they seek after some special knowledge about the newest technology. Even though technology and strategy are important, they don't hold the secret to success. God's leadership always trumps human strategy, and God's power takes technology from the realm of virtual reality to authentic life transformation.

God has provided truths through His Word, which have produced spiritual fruit in every generation. Methods and technology change, but God's Word remains the same. When these age-old truths are applied to our journey on today's Roman roads, the Holy Spirit does so much more than we could ever imagine. Truth applied to contemporary culture creates extraordinary opportunities for the gospel. There have been several biblical principles that have guided my journey.

Prayer

Prayer plays such a vital role for travel on the Roman roads that the next chapter will be completely given to this truth. However, it's important to recognize that prayer must take residence in the very heart of any strategy created to fulfill the original intent of God. The work of God must be done in the power of God. It must be done on God's timetable and under His direction. Prayer establishes our strategy and orders our steps.

Jesus instructed His disciples to wait in Jerusalem for the promise of the Father. The church was birthed in a prayer meeting as recorded in Acts 1. The Apostle Paul's ministry emerged from a prayer meeting in the thirteenth chapter. Any casual reader or student of the Book of the Acts will conclude that prayer played a critical role in the birth and advancement of the church of Jesus.

Prayer has been foundational for my ministry for many years. When I first felt called to ministry, I prayed God would never allow me to do His work in my own power. It was a dangerous prayer. God led me to difficult areas of the world where I was arrested three times for preaching the gospel. After being arrested in Romania, persecuted Christians smuggled a message to me. It read, "Don't be discouraged. God's glory comes through much suffering. Keep praying." I did. A revolution in Romania erupted one year later. I returned during the revolution and five months later preached a historical evangelistic event in a stadium. As a witness to the Romanian Revolution, I can give firsthand testimony that it wasn't just political. It was deeply spiritual. It was birthed in prayer.

Yet, more than a decade after the revolution, God spoke profoundly to my heart. While providing leadership at the Heart-Cry for Revival conference at the Billy Graham retreat center, The Cove, I experienced a personal revival. God spoke to me about my need to broaden and deepen my prayer life. Prayer had been a priority for many years prior to the Romanian Revolution. However, as my ministry grew, my prayer life did not increase proportionately. Because of the great things God did during the Romanian Revolution, it opened doors around the world for me to preach the gospel. In one week, I went from preaching in churches to preaching in stadiums.

If I was going to continue to see outpourings of God's blessings, then I couldn't stay stuck in a comfortable place of prayer. I needed to change. I was so deeply convicted about my need that I wept as I shared with the conference participants what was taking place. Ultimately, God placed it on my heart to spend three hours per day alone with Him in prayer for the seven days following the conference.

To be quite frank, I didn't have three hours a day to spare for prayer. It caused me to take a hard look at my calendar and distinguish what was really important from what was simply good. Those seven days became transformative. I realized that life's most valuable possession is time. I also understood that we all have the same amount of it—twenty-four hours in each day. I learned during those seven days that I had spent my most valuable asset with mundane matters. The exercise caused me to reevaluate my priorities, and it strengthened my prayer life. It prepared me to travel the new Roman roads that would soon thereafter be introduced to the world.

When God wants to change the course of our lives, He causes us to seek Him in ways in which we've never previously imagined. Prayer then becomes the method God uses to transform hearts, communities, and nations. Prayer releases the wind of God to blow across the sails of our souls and brings us to places we've never traveled. Prayer prepares us for the obstacles we face on the Roman roads. It leads us to those on the Roman roads who are ready to receive the gospel. Prayer opens darkened hearts with the light of the gospel. Prayer prepares the way for revival. Andrew Murray wrote, "All heaven is waiting for the prayers of His church to bring down the blessings that are stored up there for us and which God is longing to bestow."

Biblical Content

Truth transforms lives! God promises that His Word does not return void but that it accomplishes what it was sent to achieve. The technological revolution opened historical opportunities for the proclamation of the death, burial, and resurrection of Jesus. It shattered borders and enabled communication among cultures in ways that have never been possible in human history.

When Paul traveled to Thessalonica, the Bible says, "As his custom was, [Paul] went in to them, and for three Sabbaths reasoned with them from the Scriptures" (Acts 17:2). He didn't debate politics, opine about philosophy, or discuss the cultural nuances of the day. He presented the Scriptures about the death, burial, and resurrection of Jesus in a reasonable and understandable manner. And what was the result? It was said about Paul and his associates, "These who have turned the world upside down have come here too" (v. 6).

The world changed as the apostle traveled the Roman roads. But Paul made it very clear that it wasn't his "excellence of speech" (1 Corinthians 2:1) that produced the spiritual revolution in the Roman Empire. Paul's power of persuasion wasn't in his abilities but in the truth of God's Word. The presentation of Scripture in a clear and concise manner became the light that shattered the darkness.

The Protestant Reformation erupted when Martin Luther used a technological advancement to proclaim the Word of God in a manner the common person could understand. The destiny of Germany was reshaped when people were exposed to the great truths of God's Word.

Great revivals swept the early American colonies when George Whitefield stood in fields and thundered forth the Word of God. People wept. Lives changed. A nation was birthed.

I was stunned in 1980 when I first traveled to Romania. Border guards searched our luggage and inspected every inch of our van. The only things confiscated were our Bibles. Bringing Bibles into the country was equivalent to smuggling weapons or transporting pornography into the nation. I was curious why the government feared people reading an ancient book written two thousand years earlier. I learned the answer in just a couple of hours after exiting customs.

When I walked into the Emanuel Baptist Church in Oradea, I witnessed a revival similar to what I had read in early American literature. The church in Oradea was packed one hour prior to the beginning of the service. People gathered to pray and seek God. It wasn't because they had a guest speaker. No one knew we were coming. I had a similar experience everywhere we traveled in the nation. People were hungry for God's Word.

One of the churches with which I developed a strong relationship was First Baptist Church of Timisoara. I didn't know it at the time, but Timisoara would become the city where the Romanian Revolution exploded. It was in this city that I came to understand the importance and power of the proclamation of the Scriptures.

Because Bibles were confiscated in Romania, many young people gave themselves to Scripture memory. Some had memorized entire books of the Bible. Because of the confiscation of my Bible during that first entry into the country, I made it a practice to conceal the Scriptures in the secret place of my heart when I crossed the border going into Romania. When I preached, I spoke from memory.

I spoke one Sunday morning at First Baptist Church of Timisoara. It was a beautiful but chilly morning. The church was not only packed, but the outside courtyard was filled with people who shivered in the cold as they listened to the Word of God. I sensed that I wasn't communicating effectively with the people that morning. People seemed tired. The usual spirit of revival didn't seem to be permeating the congregation.

My interpreter was a young medical doctor with whom I had become close. He had memorized several books of the Bible and hundreds of individual Scriptures. He knew any verse that I wanted to quote. As I preached, I sensed I needed to stop preaching my planned message. I prayed as he translated my sentences. My mind was filled with one thought, *quote the Scriptures*. I knew my friend knew any verse that I would quote.

As I quoted the Scriptures, he started the translation before I completed the verse. It felt like we were firing a spiritual machine gun, with both of us going back and forth, quoting verse after verse. A holy silence fell on the listeners, both inside and outside. Within ten minutes, people inside wept. Then people outside cried to God. It was a moment I will never forget. It seemed as though heaven descended upon everyone inside and outside the church.

There were no clever thoughts, no great illustrations, and no deep truths—only the Word of God. Scores of people gave their hearts to Christ.

I recently spoke to the Multiplying Church movement in Brazil. My friend Pastor Fabricio had asked me to speak about using today's Roman roads to multiply disciples. More than one thousand pastors and leaders committed themselves to participate with us in developing small groups to disciple people throughout Brazil as well as conduct an evangelistic outreach in which we would present the gospel to many thousands of people. We conducted these small groups and reached out with the gospel through WhatsApp, a smartphone app that allows its users to send text and voice messages, make voice and video calls, and share images, documents, and other media.

I shared with the audience a deep concern on my heart. "I don't want to use Facebook to tell the world what I had for breakfast. I want to use Facebook to tell the world about Jesus." Many people don't realize that what they post on social media can reach multitudes living without hope. We need to be intentional about sharing the assurance, which dwells within us.

Legend says that Nero fiddled while Rome burned. Although the legend probably isn't true, the expression provides great insight into the church's attitude toward the technological revolution that is taking place. Many Christians play video games—or watch TV or scroll Instagram—while the world is scorched with sorrow. Yet the Bible is filled with help for the hopeless. It contains water that douses the flames of failure. It holds words that revive the repentant and provides medicine that heals the brokenhearted.

Christians need to develop creative social media strategies that proclaim the Word of God. Those strategies don't have to be sophisticated. They can be simple ways of getting the Word of God into the lives of people. Several years ago, I spoke in a church in Colorado. One of the men in the church asked if he could send me a daily Scripture via text messaging. I agreed, and what a blessing it has been! I don't know how he chooses the Scriptures he sends, but it seems as though every day the verse he sends is exactly what I need. On some occasions they have been very profound and have given me direction about decisions I needed to make.

God has blessed the videos and text devotions that we've placed on social media in the last two years more than I could have ever anticipated. However, I've attempted to discern the strengths and weaknesses of the discipleship materials. We place a new discipleship video and text devotion on our website and in social media every day of the year. Even though I'm speaking, I've watched all of them and prayed, "Oh, Lord, speak to my heart." I concluded after six months of watching the videos that we needed the Scriptures to be more prominent than my commentary on the Scriptures. Thus I took the second half of 2019 and created completely new daily discipleship videos that gave the Scriptures a more prominent place. We began using them in 2020. We know that the impact will be much more profound in the lives of people because the Bible says, "For the word of God is living and powerful, and sharper than any two-edged sword, piercing even to the division of soul and spirit, and of joints and marrow, and is a discerner of the thoughts and intents of the heart" (Hebrews 4:12). After years of traveling the Roman roads, Paul told young Timothy, "Preach the word!" (2 Timothy 4:2).

Community

Many mistakenly believe what is needed for a successful ministry is merely a cool set of apps and a nice-looking website. Yet the best delivery method in the technological world can never be a substitute for authentic human relationships. Virtual relationships should never replace real relationships.

Social media should enhance social interaction rather than curtail it.

Paul wrote to the church at Thessalonica that his ministry to them was not simply a matter of delivering the Word of God to them. He proved his authenticity by the manner in which he lived (1 Thessalonians 1:5).

One of the greatest things that transpired during the last few years since I began traveling on the modern Roman roads is that I've built stronger relationships with Christian friends around the world. Social media and technology tools have enabled me to strengthen my relationships. For instance, I've not been in India in the last three years, but my relationship with Pastor Jolly has grown stronger and deeper.

There's one simple reason: communication. All strong relationships in families, churches, or businesses must be built on effective communication. This generation has been blessed with extraordinary communication tools that allow strong relationships to be built. I can honestly say that I've become closer to Pastor Jolly in India and Pastor Fabricio in Brazil because I've been able to communicate with them more often and more effectively by using technology tools such as Skype, Zoom, and WhatsApp. I've had phone conversations with Pastor Jolly in India on almost a weekly basis. Not only have we discussed ministry, but we've also discussed more personal things such as family life, time management, and how to handle disappointments. Yet today's Roman roads have not only enhanced my relationship with friends; I've learned that powerful ministry on the Roman roads can be built upon established relationships.

When I celebrated forty years of evangelistic ministry, I sought God for direction for the next season of my life and ministry. He placed on my heart that I needed to meet with some younger evangelists and teach them what I had learned about doing the work of the evangelist. I didn't stop preaching evangelistic events. Rather I took time after those events to spend a few days with younger men who had a heart for evangelism and teach them what I had learned during the previous forty years of ministry.

It was then I met with younger men in India, Brazil, and Africa. We began a mentoring relationship that has continued and grown during the past twelve years. As technology and social media expanded, I was able to not only help my friends with their ministries, but they were able to help me understand the capacity of the new Roman roads to reach people beyond anything I had ever imagined. Consequently, we've been able to reach more people with the gospel in a few short years than I did in the past fifty.

We've seen success because we have had strong relationships.

We've not only used technology to enhance our communication with each other, but we've been able to reach millions of people because of such strong relationships.

Many Christians fail at using technology because they only view it as a quick and cheap way to market their church, ministry, or organization.

My relationship with Pastor Fabricio began in Brazil long before I personally met him. Several years after I met him, I preached an evangelistic meeting in Brasilia, the capital of the nation and the city where Pastor Fabricio lived and worked. It was then that he first worked with our outreach. Our relationship was birthed. Today he serves as executive director of evangelism for the National Mission Board of the Brazilian Baptist Convention and as a leader in the Multiplying Church Movement in Brazil. When he became the executive director of evangelism, he shared his burden for families in the country because the family was under attack in Brazil (as it is in many countries).

The National Mission Board published my book *Praying for Your Family,* and Pastor Fabricio and I traveled throughout Brazil for several years encouraging people to learn to pray for and minister to their families. However, once we began to travel on the twenty-first century Roman roads, the ministry erupted in spiritual multiplication.

In October 2018, Pastor Fabricio asked if I could provide him with thirty-one videos about praying for your family. I did so, and the Multiplying Church movement created curriculum for adults and children for each of the videos. They then distributed them to tens of thousands of people clustered in small groups via WhatsApp during May 2019.

Pastor Fabricio had thirty-three key pastors he mentored and connected with through WhatsApp. Each of those pastors had up to sixty-six pastors they mentored and connected with via WhatsApp. Each of those two thousand pastors had ten to twenty small group leaders in their church whom they mentored and connected with through WhatsApp. Each of the small group leaders had twenty to thirty people in their small groups. If you add and multiply those numbers of people, you have hundreds of thousands of people involved in small group discipleship. There were large numbers of people who were accountable to someone in a small group. It was through these small groups that we released the *Praying for Your Family* videos and curriculum. We used technology, but the power of the technology was built upon human relationships. Many thousands of families were helped not only by the resources but also by small group relationships.

Technology ministry built upon strong human relationships has the potential to reach far beyond geographical, political, and religious barriers. A church that has an ethnic community within its sphere of their local church community has the capacity to reach hundreds and even thousands of people from the national origin of that ethnic community. The world has changed. The world is in the world. God has brought the world to the world. Those who understand how to build relationships and use technology can reach the world for Christ.

One pastor in Indiana understood this principle and brought on to his staff Wycliff Keter, a man from Kenya who had married one of the young women in his church. The church now has a deep and widespread outreach into Kenya because of that one relationship, and it now has a formal relationship with 2,500 churches in East Africa. Relationships create new relationships.

However, many of us are like the blind man Jesus healed outside of Bethsaida. When he was first healed, he saw people as trees—inanimate objects. Jesus placed His hand upon the man's eyes a second time, and the man saw people clearly. (See Mark 8:22–26.) Likewise, God has placed people all around us. We often don't see them as He sees them. We need a fresh touch from heaven to see the people around us as they are. When that takes place, the resulting relationships have the potential to change the world.

Consistency

A successful ministry event on the Roman roads doesn't necessarily produce lasting fruit. However, consistency of life tied to the proclamation of the gospel will create successful events, which yield permanent fruit. Consistency is one of the most powerful success principles in life. The person who "walks the walk" will always have an advantage over the person who only "talks the talk." Paul told the church at Corinth, "My speech and my preaching were not with persuasive words of human wisdom, but in demonstration of the Spirit and of power, that your faith should not be in the wisdom of men but in the power of God" (1 Corinthians 2:4). Paul understood that consistent living was the result of God's power at work in the human heart to produce genuine faith.

There's also another kind of consistency that God blesses—consistency of activity. It could be called the power of purposeful repetition. Jesus said, "You have been faithful over a few things, I will make you ruler over many things" (Matthew 25:23). This truth is reiterated throughout the Bible. The Book of Hebrews warns Christians not to forsake "the assembling of ourselves together, as is the manner of some," but to instead engage in "exhorting one another, and so much the more as you see the Day approaching" (Hebrews 10:25). Meeting with other believers on a consistent basis is critical to successful Christian living.

This truth is especially true on the Roman roads. One of the reasons Paul had so much success was because he didn't have an "event" mentality. Don't misunderstand. Events took place—powerful ones that brought many into the kingdom of God. However, the goal was never to conduct great events on the Roman roads. The goal was always to produce disciples who could also make disciples. That meant he needed to not only go to a city to proclaim the gospel but also to return there. His letters to the churches constituted another method in which he could continue to have input into their lives.

This is why churches conduct worship services on a weekly basis. It's why athletes work out daily. It's why businesses have daily work schedules. It takes work that is strategic, smart, and must be done on a consistent basis.

When I first investigated using social media as a major outreach strategy, I talked with Jerry Smith, the executive pastor at my home church. Alamo City Church was using social media to reach many more people than just those who attended on Sunday. It was impressive how the church not only encouraged people to watch the Sunday services but how Alamo City reached out and ministered to those who watched. They built relationships, which enabled ministry. I asked Jerry about the success of the church's social media ministry, and he gave me much insight. But one of the things he repeated often was, "Be consistent."

I took his advice. That's why we have a short video every day. Instead of trying to feed people a five-course meal all at once, we try to give them one course at a time. Five of my short devotions might equal one Sunday morning message for a pastor. However, through social media posts, I'm able to help build consistency into the lives of those watching. One of the primary goals of our outreach is to help believers develop a daily time alone with God. If we can provide a resource that is delivered in a timely manner on a consistent basis, it will help Christians develop consistency in their walks with God.

It's worked. At the time of this writing, we are producing daily discipleship videos for eleven language groups and averaging 6.5 million views per month. There's nothing deep about my teaching on the videos. They are simple teachings on how to walk with God. They aren't professionally filmed. I record them on my iPhone with a microphone attached. Most of the time, I record them in my office with no assistance. If I go outside my office, my daughter helps with the filming. Because the videos appear daily, our pages have developed large followings. People need and want consistency.

Prayer, the Word of God, strong relationships, and consistency create an incredible vehicle, which enables us to travel to far away destinations on the Roman roads.

Chapter 7
The Power of Prayer

~~~~~~~

And Barnabas and Saul returned from Jerusalem when they had fulfilled their ministry, and they also took with them John whose surname was Mark. Now in the church that was at Antioch there were certain prophets and teachers: Barnabas, Simeon who was called Niger, Lucius of Cyrene, Manaen who had been brought up with Herod the tetrarch, and Saul. As they ministered to the Lord and fasted, the Holy Spirit said, "Now separate to Me Barnabas and Saul for the work to which I have called them." Then, having fasted and prayed, and laid hands on them, they sent them away.
—Acts 12:25—13:1–3

God has placed a group of men around me who are not only dear friends but also serve as the board of directors of Sammy Tippit Ministries. They encourage me as well as hold me accountable in my personal walk with God and ministry to the world. I often discuss with them the concepts that are on my heart because I place high value on their insights. During one of our times together, we had a discussion about the rapid growth and multiplication of the church as recorded in the Book of Acts.

One of the men asked a question that took residence in my heart until I could find an answer. He asked, "Was it feasible for the church to continue to multiply throughout the entire Book of Acts? Could it maintain such high intensity of growth?" He pointed out that Acts 12:24 was the last time that the word *multiply* had been used.

I pondered the question for nearly a year as I read and searched Scripture. One morning the answer became so clear that I chuckled and wondered how I could have missed it for so long. What we see when we read the Bible today is not exactly what was seen by believers who read those early manuscripts. The original biblical manuscripts didn't contain chapter and verse breaks. They were written as documents and would be seen much more like a modern-day letter. The chapter and verse numbers were given later for the purpose of convenience. Those breaks are for our benefit because they enable us to find portions of Scriptures quickly and allow us to cross-reference different passages of the Bible that contain the same stream of thought.

Yet it's very important to keep in mind the context of the book we are reading. In this case, it's also important to follow the flow of the text within the book. In Acts 12:24, we have a record of the explosive growth of the church in Jerusalem. Then the focus changes two verses later (Acts 13:1) to a prayer meeting in Antioch. Most of the remainder of the Book of Acts chronicles Paul taking the gospel to the non-Jewish world. The question then becomes, "What happened between the explosive growth in Jerusalem and the prayer meeting in Antioch?" We only have one short verse that gives us any indication. It says, "And Barnabas and Saul returned from Jerusalem when they had fulfilled their ministry, and they also took with them John whose surname was Mark" (Acts 12:25). When we read the Book of Acts as the early Christians would have read it, we understand that this report wasn't just filler for the manuscript. It was an important transitional statement because the entire focus was going to change from this moment in the manuscript until the end of the Book of Acts.

Several questions need to be asked. What happened to Saul and Barnabas as they traveled from Jerusalem to Antioch? What did they experience? And what did they think about what they had encountered? Did their trip have any impact on what transpired in Antioch? No one knows exactly what they saw. My guess is that there was nothing extraordinary about what they experienced. If something significant had transpired, Luke probably would have recorded it. However, we do have a general idea of what they would have seen, and we have some very good evidence of the thoughts of Saul (who, after the prayer meeting in Antioch, become known as the Apostle Paul).

Remember the road to Antioch would have been filled with all sorts of people—from gladiators to senators, dancing girls to philosophers, and merchants with spices to religious leaders with idols. What were Saul's thoughts? How did he react to them? There's no exact and definitive answer to those questions. However, we do have an idea of his thinking process and heart attitude because of what he wrote in his epistles to the churches.

To some extent, all of us are shaped by our surroundings. There's no doubt Saul would have been impacted by what he saw on the way to Antioch and even after he arrived in the city. He saw a plethora of cultures and types of people. He was convinced Jesus loved them, no matter their lifestyle or background. They needed salvation, deliverance, and forgiveness that only Jesus could provide.

He described himself as the *chief of sinners* (1 Timothy 1:15). He had experienced God's grace and felt a deep burden to share this good news with those he encountered. We know this heart attitude dwelt deep within because he later wrote to the church at Rome, "I am a debtor both to Greeks and to barbarians, both to wise and to unwise" (Romans 1:14). That statement gives us insight into what he must have felt as he traveled to Antioch and remained with the believers there. He knew the good news was for all people—whether Greeks or foreigners, educated or uneducated. Every person deserved to hear the good news of God's love and salvation.

Saul walked into a prayer meeting having seen a lost and dying world and came out as Paul, a man with a mandate to share the gospel with all people, everywhere. That's the transition we see in the Book of Acts. The outpouring of God's Spirit was never intended to be limited to the saints in Jerusalem. The purpose of the work of the Holy Spirit was to enable the church to fulfill the original intent of God. The prayer meeting in Antioch transformed Paul's burden *for* the world into his mission *into* the world. The rest of the Book of Acts has its focus on that mission. From that point forward, we see Paul on the Roman roads or in a ship with a lateen sail taking him to some faraway place to tell others about the love of Jesus and help them to grow in God's grace.

The great works of God, both in Jerusalem on the day of Pentecost and in Antioch on the day that Paul was commissioned as an apostle to the Gentiles, were birthed in prayer meetings. Prayer is the common thread throughout the Book of Acts. When believers cried to God, the church spread rapidly throughout the Roman Empire.

Prayer Returns Us to the Promises in God's Word

The thrust of the church took place in two cities: Jerusalem and Antioch. These two cities had three things in common with each other. First, a great movement of the Holy Spirit had been birthed in prayer. Second, both prayer meetings resulted in powerful proclamations of the gospel. Third, the results of prayer multiplied the church. We see God bringing His people back to His original intent in Jerusalem and Antioch. He brought people from around the world to Jerusalem in that historic moment when the Holy Spirit was poured upon the believers. And He sent a small band of men from Antioch with passionate hearts to proclaim the good news of God's love to people around the world.

In both instances, prayer brought God's people back to His original intent. Prayer produced deep love in the hearts of believers. Prayer is the communion of two hearts—the heart of God and the heart of man. When we embrace His heart in prayer, we will want what is on His heart. And what's on His heart? *The world! The world is on the heart of God!* That has never changed and never will. We often become so involved with the worries of the world that we lose sight of the heart of God to save those in the world. Yet, if we will seek Him, we will surely find Him. We'll be renewed by the love that has been in His heart since the beginning of time.

When the love of God floods our souls, we will have the courage of Peter and the power of Paul. Our hearts will burn with an ancient fire—the fire of God's love for a lost and dying world.

It's the same fire that has changed the course of history, launched reformations, and ignited spiritual revivals. When this fire spreads, it brings life and growth rather than death and destruction.

The fire of God swept through Monroe, Louisiana, in February 1970. A godly pastor, L. L. Morris, asked God to send fire from heaven among the youth of his church. Most of them had left the church, and Pastor Morris's heart broke. The praying pastor asked me to lead a series of youth rallies. He set a meeting, but only a handful came. I told Pastor Morris that I didn't think we should go forward because of the lack of interest. However, I saw a twinkle in his eyes. He smiled and said, "I've been praying. And God is going to work among our young people."

I had a difficult time believing God would work in that situation. Only about twenty-five people attended the first night. No one responded during the time in which I invited people to give their lives to Christ. I wanted to tell the pastor that we shouldn't continue the meetings, but I saw the smile on his face and the twinkle in his eyes. I knew to keep quiet.

The Holy Spirit worked quietly in the hearts of the small group who attended the following evening. Almost everyone was at the altar at the front of the church seeking God as the service concluded. The church was packed the following evening. People came to Christ. By the final night of the week, the church had the largest crowd in its history. The fire of God fell on the youth.

I once again saw the twinkle in Pastor Morris's eyes as he said we needed to extend the meetings for another week. We did, but we had to move out of the church because the crowds had grown so much. We moved on to the college campus. Then we had to move again. More and more people attended nightly. By the end of the meetings, we were in the Civic Center. Drug addicts came to Christ and were set free. The fire of God spread through the university campus. Students were set aflame with the love of Christ.

We set up a place of prayer at a local Christian coffeehouse. Young people could be found there seeking God twenty-four hours a day. During those days, I couldn't eat because I was so caught up in the movement of the Spirit of God. It was a moment in which it seemed like time had stopped and heaven visited Monroe. Those days began with a simple pastor, a man who believed the Ancient of Days still visited His people. He held fast to a conviction that God would hear and answer his prayers. He believed in the power of the proclamation of the gospel. He held to those ancient promises that God revives those who humble themselves and pray and seek His face and turn from their wicked ways (2 Chronicles 7:14).

God's heart has not changed. His truths remain steadfast. The prayer meetings in Jerusalem and Antioch revived the vision of simple, humble men and women to fulfill God's original intent. God still revives. When men and women like Pastor Morris seek Him, He will answer. The grand old promises of God's Word will become wonderful new realities in our lives.

Prayer Forges the Future

The prayer meetings in Jerusalem and Antioch not only gave those early believers a fresh vision of the God of Abraham, Isaac, and Jacob, but they also thrust them into a new world and showed them how to make a difference in it. Fishermen became fishers of men. Doubters dared to dream about new roads to travel in order to proclaim the death, burial, and resurrection of Jesus. Believers became unstoppable. Many were persecuted. Some fled their homes. Paul was run out of town. Yet they refused to give up. They forged ahead with a fearless faith. They kept their eyes on Jesus.

After the Apostle Paul was sent from the prayer meeting in Antioch to proclaim the gospel among the Gentiles, he traveled to Philippi. How would he reach the people? What would be his strategy? How could he fulfill the original intent of God? For him, the strategy was simple. Pray, proclaim the gospel, and make disciples. After staying in the city for a few days, he went outside the city by the river where Jewish people gathered for prayer. He could not forget the power of prayer he experienced in Antioch.

A businesswoman came to faith in Christ at that place of prayer. Her entire family became followers of Jesus, and they were baptized (Acts 16:13–15). Paul went to the place of prayer, proclaimed the gospel, and then spent time with those who came to Christ, teaching the Word of God.

Not only did the businesswoman come to Christ, but a demon-possessed girl was also set free from the darkness that filled her heart. The men who had abused the young woman became incensed because they lost their financial gains that had resulted from their control over her. They brought Paul and Silas before the authorities and had them arrested and thrown into prison (vv. 16–24).

How did Paul respond? He could no longer go to the place of prayer because he was confined to a dungeon. How would he now fulfill the original intent of God? He prayed. He proclaimed the gospel. He made disciples. Nothing changed. As he and Silas worshipped the Savior, God sent an earthquake, and the jailer came to Christ (vv. 25–34). Paul prayed no matter the situation. That's how he began, and that's how he would continue to fulfill the original intent of God. Prayer opened doors—even prison doors. As he prayed, God showed him what to do and where to go. As he continued to pray, people came to Christ. When he persisted in prayer, God worked miracles. Prayer forged his future and enabled him to fulfill God's plan.

If we seek God when the future looks dark and God's plan seems impossible, God will answer in extraordinary ways. He turns darkness to light, transforms despair into hope, and creates a path in the wilderness. He shows us the way forward when we face impossible walls.

I first saw the Berlin Wall in 1972. My heart broke. Soldiers with machines guns camped in towers every two hundred meters. They had orders to shoot any of their fellow countrymen in East Germany who dared to attempt to escape to West Berlin. East Berlin looked like a giant prison. My wife and I would go to the wall each evening and pray an impossible prayer. "Oh, God, open the doors for the gospel. Help me to bring the good news of Your love to the people who have no opportunity to hear about You."

The reason my request seemed impossible to have an answer was because of what had transpired during the years of communism. Young people at the age of fourteen were forced to choose between the "Free German Youth" (the communist youth organization) and the church. If they chose the church, their educational opportunities became limited. Consequently, young people left the church en masse. Huge cathedrals were empty, with only a handful of elderly attending.

After much prayer, two friends and I decided to infiltrate a communist youth festival in 1973 to share the gospel. More than 100,000 atheist and communist youth were expected to attend the meeting in East Berlin. Even though the idea seemed impossible, God gave us promises from His Word that produced hope. We not only saw God work miracles as we daily crossed the border from West Berlin to East Berlin, but God opened hearts to the gospel when we arrived at the meeting. We led more than two hundred communist youth to faith in Christ. The entire story is detailed in my autobiography, *Unashamed: A Memoir of Dangerous Faith.*

One of the most amazing things that took place in Alexanderplatz, the place where the communist youth gathered each evening, was when we met Christian youth. They had prayed and asked God to lead them to Christians from other parts of the world. When we showed up and shared Christ, they joined us. What we learned from them was what astounded me.

A few years before we went to the communist youth festival, an East German pastor's heart broke for the young people of his country. He started a Bible study for the youth in his village. However, none were interested. He didn't know what to do. Yet he knew what had transpired in the prayer meetings in Jerusalem and Antioch. Therefore he and a friend decided to seek God. They met together in prayer once each week for a year. Then they spent fourteen days in prayer and fasting. At the close of that time, they once again attempted to start a Bible study with the youth of the village.

More than sixty young people attended that first meeting. It grew to one hundred, then two hundred, and later to five hundred. Young people were traveling from all over East Germany to attend the Bible studies. It grew to fifteen hundred. So many were coming that they started meeting in five locations, most of them in the major urban centers of the country.

These Christian young people who came to the communist youth festival invited my colleagues and me to visit the growing Christian youth meetings. I went to two of them, one in Leipzig and the other in Dresden. I was asked to speak at the one in Dresden. I was shocked at what I witnessed. More than two thousand youth filled the huge cathedral in Dresden to worship Jesus. Once the service concluded, they left and another two thousand youth filled the building to hear the Word of God and learn how to follow Jesus.

God transformed a generation because of one pastor in a small village. When all seemed impossible, he prayed. He knew the future of an entire generation could be forged through prayer. He prayed. He proclaimed. He made disciples. And the Berlin wall came down.

Prayer Releases the Glory of God

When Jesus taught His disciples about prayer, He concluded by telling them to pray, "For Yours is the kingdom and the power and the glory forever. Amen" (Matthew 6:13). The target for which we pray should be the glory of God. True prayer replaces our ministries, strengths, and egos with His power, His kingdom, and His glory.

Powerful praying is kingdom praying. If we're going to see a mighty outpouring of God's Spirit in this generation, we must pray with hearts that long for the King to reign in the hearts of people. Our hearts must long for the kingdom of God rather than our empires. He is not interested in building our ministries and creating large organizations. His desire is for His rule, reign, and love to flood the hearts of men and women everywhere. He longs to have a relationship with people. That's why Jesus came to earth. Prayer releases the kingdom of God to come to earth and the will of God to be done in the hearts of people.

Kingdom work is spiritual work and cannot be accomplished by the power of human effort. It requires God's power to change human hearts. It was critically important for Paul to travel the Roman roads and get in a ship with a lateen sail to bring the good news to distant shores. Without arriving at those destinations, he had no opportunity to see God's original intent fulfilled. Yet he knew that the work of God had to be done by the power of the Spirit of God. He wrote, "And my speech and my preaching were not with persuasive words of human wisdom, but in demonstration of the Spirit and of power" (1 Corinthians 2:4).

One of the greatest lessons I needed to learn as a new believer was that it was not my speaking abilities that would bring people into God's kingdom. It was not my ability to persuade but rather God's power to transform that was critically important in seeing God's kingdom come and His will being done. That meant prayer had to be foundational in the work to which I had been called.

When we pray for the kingdom to come and make ourselves available for the power of God, then we position ourselves to see the glory of God. We set our sails and are ready for the wind of God to blow across our hearts, families, and communities. We become a generation that seeks the presence of the king of glory. The psalmist wrote about lifting our heads and doors so that the King of glory could come in. When the King of glory comes, that's revival. It is the presence of God among the people of God. When the King of glory comes, everything changes. Our lives will be turned right side up. Our hurts will be healed, our communities transformed, and our eyes will behold the majesty and splendor of God.

There have been a few instances in which my eyes have beheld the glory of God among the people of God. One of them was in Romania during the revolution. The revolution in the country began with a praying pastor in the city of Oradea. He taught his people to pray in an unusual manner during the mid-1970s. He instructed them to pray that one day they would stand in the great stadiums and proclaim the gospel—that they would preach on television and radio.

People said, "Pastor, that's impossible. We're persecuted for our faith. We lose our jobs and our educational opportunities. Some of us have gone to prison."

Yet, the pastor told them, "With God nothing is impossible."

The people prayed—not for one year, not even five years. They prayed for fifteen years for the glory of God. I will never forget the first time I visited the Emanuel Baptist Church in Oradea. It was packed with people praying an hour before the beginning of the service. A revival spread throughout that region of the country. However, the more the people prayed, the darker the days became. Persecution increased to such an extent that the US Ambassador to

Romania, Dr. David Funderburk, resigned in 1985 in protest of the persecution of the Christians in the country.

I traveled throughout the country preaching from 1980 to 1988. However, I was arrested in 1988 and put out of the country. Border guards told me that I would never be allowed back into the country. They said I would never place my feet on Romanian soil as long as I lived. However, there was something they didn't know. *God is on His throne, and He orders the affairs of human history!*

Christians persisted in prayer. Then an evangelical pastor in Timisoara was to be arrested in December 1989. Christians surrounded his apartment to protect him. The crowds grew daily. The Securitate (the Romanian secret police) shot into the crowd, killing innocent men, women, and children. Tens of thousands of people gathered in the main square to protest the slaughter of those innocent people. A pastor friend of mine preached to the multitudes, and in one divine moment, the King of glory came into Romania.

The crowd, which was made up of people who had been taught scientific atheism all their lives, shouted, *"Există Dumnezeu! Există Dumnezeu!"* (There is a God! There is a God!) This scene spread to the major metropolitan centers of the country. Romanian friends sent a message to me saying, "Sammy, that for which we have prayed for so many years has finally transpired. You must return to the country."

I left everything I was doing, caught a plane, and flew to Vienna, Austria, where friends picked me up and traveled with me to Romania. We didn't know what to expect when we arrived at the border. Before the revolution, the first question asked at the border was always, "Do you have any Bibles?" If you had Bibles, you had problems. I'll never forget that night, January 1, 1990, as long as I live. The snow was falling. We were the only ones attempting to enter the country. Everyone else was trying to leave. It was dark. It was cold. The revolution was still in progress. The border guards approached and told us to get out of the car. We didn't know who was in charge of the border. One of the guards then asked, "Are you Christians?"

I felt like my heart had climbed into my throat. "Yes," I stuttered. "We're Christians."

The border guard threw his arms open wide and exclaimed, "Welcome to the new Romania!" A Romanian friend had been waiting for us at the customs office. He ran out to meet us. We embraced. We wept. We prayed. We gave glory to God. When we arrived in the country, flags flew everywhere. However, they had a hole cut in the middle of them. They had removed the symbol of communism. Romania would never be the same. The King of glory had visited the country. And one pastor's prayers had been answered.

Chapter 8

Multiplying Disciples through Discipleship and Evangelism

~~~

"Go therefore and make disciples of all the nations, baptizing them in the name of the Father and of the Son and of the Holy Spirit, teaching them to observe all things that I have commanded you; and lo, I am with you always, even to the end of the age." Amen. —Matthew 28:19–20

The awakening in Romania may have been the most significant move of God's Spirit in the late twentieth century, but what God is doing in Iran today may be the greatest revival of the early twenty-first century. Much of my thinking about the relationship between innovation and revival has resulted from my interaction with Persian believers during the past twenty years. It's truly mind-boggling what God is doing in Iran.

The first time that I came in contact with God's work in the Persian world was in 1998. I was speaking at a pastors' conference in California when one of the leaders of the Jesus Film Project challenged me to go to Iran and pray for God to open doors for the gospel inside the country. After much discussion, I agreed to go. He then told me that Americans were banned from travel to Iran. I laughed as I told him, "You want me to go to Iran to pray for God to open doors for the gospel, but I must first pray for God to open doors to get into Iran so that I can pray for God to open doors?"

I agreed to go once Americans were allowed into the country. He called me a few months later asking, "Are you ready to go to Iran?"

We traveled to the country and spent ten days in prayer. Our only objective was to seek God for the nation. We walked the streets of the country and cried to God on behalf of the Persian people. One day, as I had just completed walking in Imam Square in Isfahan, I asked God how the gospel could get into a country so controlled by Islam. I then looked up and saw the answer on top of the apartment buildings. Satellite dishes covered the rooftops. *That's it*, I thought. *The message of the gospel can reach deep into the hearts of the people through satellite technology.*

I shared what had taken place with my colleague from the Jesus Film Project. We agreed in prayer, asking God to open the doors for the gospel to infiltrate the nation through satellite television. My friend approached me a few months later and asked, "Would you like to begin a satellite television broadcast into Iran?" He told me that an Iranian pastor had begun broadcasting into Iran. He was interested in talking with me about the possibility of reaching into the country via satellite television with the gospel. We joined him in his vision, and God has done so much more than we could have ever imagined. I'll never forget the first time I spoke into the country through satellite television. I joined the Iranian pastor in his studio, and we produced a live broadcast into the country.

I briefly shared my testimony of how I came to Christ. I wasn't prepared for what took place within the following few minutes. The phone lines lit up. Scores of people inside Iran called into the studio in California. They wept. Their lives were empty and their problems immense. They sought help. We shared the gospel and prayed with them late into the night. After we concluded, people continued calling. I was completely exhausted when I left the studio. I had no idea how hungry and open the Persian people were for the gospel. That began several years of ministry by using satellite television.

A few years later, Lazarus Yeghnazar, president of 222 Ministries, also asked me to participate with him in his television broadcast into Iran. Lazarus had been reared in the Assembly of God church in Tehran. He and his brothers live in England and America, and all of them have different but wonderful ministries among the Persian people. Lazarus told me one day, "When I was a young man living in Iran, I thought we were experiencing revival in our church if we had two people in a year come to Christ. Now, thousands upon thousands of people in Iran are coming to Christ."

I traveled to Turkey a few years ago to meet with Persian refugees. Many Iranian Christians had fled the country because of severe persecution. Their stories amazed me. When they arrived in Turkey, they immediately started gathering in homes and sharing Jesus. Consequently, numerous house churches were birthed. One of the young men asked me, "Can you help us develop an app for mobile devices to disciple the new believers? So many people are coming to Christ. We need to help them to grow in their faith."

When I returned to the United States, I set on a journey to discover how to effectively use technology to reach the Persian world. That's when I came in contact with the software designer Herman Spencer. It was then that he told me, "You dream. Then you tell me what your dream is, and we will find a way to accomplish it."

My dream was a simple one: *discipleship and evangelism*. I knew the power of this biblical truth and also knew that it was desperately needed in the fast-growing Persian-Christian community.

What Is Discipleship and Evangelism?

Both terms, *discipleship* and *evangelism,* are strong New Testament concepts. Just before Jesus ascended to heaven, He told His followers to "make disciples of all the nations" and teach the new disciples to observe all things He had commanded (Matthew 28:19–20). He told them to make disciples who would make disciples—who would make disciples. The word *disciple* stems from a Greek word, *mathétés,* which is used in some form more than 250 times in the Gospels and the Book of Acts.

Jesus called people to follow Him, and those who followed became known as disciples. He explained the nature of a true disciple in John 15 when He spoke of an abiding relationship. He said a true disciple is one who abides (dwells, lives) in Him and bears fruit as a result of that continuing intimacy with God. Thus a disciple is one who walks with Christ, developing an ongoing relationship with Him. He consistently told those who wanted to follow Him that there was a price to be paid to be His disciple.

A disciple of Jesus is a person who believes in Jesus and is committed to learning, growing, and becoming more like Him. Discipleship is a process that begins when the human heart is transformed from one that is self-indulgent to a Christ-centered heart. The new birth initiates spiritual growth in those who have placed their faith in Jesus.

Evangelism comes from the Greek word *euaggelion*, from which we have the word "gospel" or "good news" or "good telling." The four accounts of the life of Jesus are called Gospels because they tell the ultimate good news, the story of the One who stepped out of eternity into human history, the eternal God who took upon Himself human flesh to live a holy, sinless, perfect life. It tells the good news that He took the punishment for our sins when He died on the Cross and rose from the grave three days later. It brings good news of hope for the hopeless, forgiveness for the guilty, and freedom for the spiritually captive.

When we read the Gospel accounts, we don't find evangelism (good news telling) as a truth that is opposed to or apart from discipleship (learning and growing in Christ). The biblical texts never present them as contrary to one another. Yet that is exactly what has happened in much of the Christian world today, especially in the West. We've somehow created a schism between two great truths. Evangelism is good news telling while discipleship is embracing the good news by following and learning of the One who is the good news.

The Problem of Discipleship without Evangelism

Two problems exist when there is an imbalance of discipleship without evangelism. First, it's impossible to make genuine disciples of Jesus without *good news telling*. The disciple of Jesus longs to be like Him. A true follower of Jesus longs to grow into His image. The disciple is above all else a learner, one who is in the process of learning how to live and love like Jesus lived and loved. The central question for the disciple becomes, "Why did Jesus come to this planet? What was His goal?"

If we are going to be like Jesus, then we must give ourselves to the central objective of His life. It's no secret why He came. He told those who followed Him, "For the Son of Man has come to save that which was lost" (Matthew 18:11). He then spoke a parable about a shepherd going after a sheep that had gone astray. There wasn't any doubt in the minds of those early followers of what Jesus meant. They gave their lives to bring people to Christ.

Most of them died because they were *good news* tellers. They traveled the Roman roads and sailed on ships to tell the world the good news that God had clothed Himself with human flesh and that He lived a sinless, holy life. These common, ordinary men and women declared that Jesus died to take the punishment for our sins, that He was buried in a borrowed tomb, and that He arose from the dead three days later. They boldly proclaimed that Jesus had overcome every enemy of humanity—sin, death, hell, and the devil. And they died doing it! Good news telling was at the center of the heart of the early disciples of Jesus. A true disciple of Jesus today will have a passion to share the good news.

The second problem of discipleship void of evangelism is that it produces a type of *comfortable Christianity.* One of the interesting observations I've made during the last fifty years is that the great outpourings of the Holy Spirit have taken place where Christians suffer much. The revival in Romania took place during great persecution from the communists. The move of God's Spirit in the Persian world has been accompanied by scores of Christians being thrown in prison. The strong arm of the Chinese government has come down on the rapidly growing Chinese church.

Suffering was a major characteristic of the early followers of Jesus. The church at Antioch grew because Christians had been scattered due to persecution. When the Apostle Paul was in prison, he wrote to the church at Philippi, "I also count all things loss for the excellence of the knowledge of Christ Jesus my Lord, for whom I have suffered the loss of all things, and count them as rubbish, that I may gain Christ and be found in Him . . . that I may know Him and the power of His resurrection, and the fellowship of His sufferings, being conformed to His death" (Philippians 3:8, 10).

Paul and the early Christians knew nothing of comfortable Christianity. Why was Paul in prison? He told the good news to people everywhere. *He could have lived comfortably in the confines of the Christian community. But he didn't. He chose the way of the Cross. He caught a ride on a ship, traveled the Roman roads, and told the good news everywhere he went.*

But it wasn't only Paul. According to Indian tradition, Thomas traveled to the Chennai region in India and declared the good news. He was put to death for his evangelistic work. Strong Christian tradition says the Apostle Peter was placed in prison in Rome and put to death. It's believed that each of the original disciples, with the exception of the Apostle John, author of the Book of Revelation, died a martyr's death telling the good news. Comfortable Christianity was never a part of discipleship in early Christianity. Nor is it today.

It's easy to stay within the comfort zone of fellowship with other Christians. There's no threat there. It's a safe place. However, when our passion is to become like Jesus, we will fervently seek to save those who are lost. We'll move out of our comfort zones and into heavenly battle zones. We'll enroll in the school of discipleship that takes us into the battle for the souls of people everywhere.

The Problem of Evangelism without Discipleship

After having studied the great historical revivals and also having been a firsthand witness to awakenings during the Jesus Movement in America, the revival in Romania, and now the outpouring of God's Spirit in the Persian world, I've observed some shortcomings in revivals. Spiritual imbalance is perhaps the greatest threat to the continuation of any spiritual awakening. The purpose of revival is to return us to the highway of holiness. It's easy to embrace one aspect of Christlikeness and neglect the other.

Two Christlike character qualities have consistently driven God's people to pray for revival: love and holiness. When Christians see their families, friends, and colleagues through the eyes of God's love, they are compelled to share the good news with them. On the other hand, when believers see themselves in the light of God's holiness, they are urged by the Holy Spirit to humble themselves and seek God for change in their lives—to be more like Christ. Thus they renew themselves to growth in Christ. Discipleship takes center stage in their lives because holiness is the process of becoming like Jesus.

It's important to remember that we need both characteristics of Christ—love and holiness. If we only embrace one, we become imbalanced. If I were to paint a perfect picture of your face, but drew your ears disproportionately larger than the rest of your face, I would have created a monster. That's often what happens when we exaggerate one great truth about Jesus over another. This is perhaps the greatest temptation for those who have been consumed with the love of God. They often lose sight of God's holiness.

Evangelism without discipleship also has two major flaws. First, it has the potential to produce a strange kind of disciple. Second, it will never impact the culture in a transformative manner. One of the great aspects of the good news is that God has provided a way for us to have a personal relationship with Him, the One who is holy. However, He loves us too much to only forgive us from our sins. He loves us enough to deliver us from any and all of our character flaws. He loves us so much that He would never leave us the way He found us. His desire is to conform us into the image of His Son (Romans 8:29). If we only proclaim the good news of God's forgiveness, we've proclaimed only half the story. Jesus died on the Cross to forgive us, but He arose from the grave to transform us.

Transformation begins at the moment of our spiritual birth but continues throughout our Christian lives. The Holy Spirit comes to live within us the moment we place our faith in Jesus. Then we have the power of God dwelling within us, which means we have the power to change. We've been set free from the chains, but we need to learn to live with this newly found freedom.

This is why Paul traveled the Roman roads. It's why he returned to Rome. It's why we find that he not only proclaimed the good news, but he also wrote letters to those who came to Christ, encouraging them to grow in their faith. It's why he returned to many of the other places where people had come to Christ. He knew the importance of discipleship. The normal Christian life is the one that is continually being transformed into the image of Jesus. It's a life given to the command that Jesus gave His followers. Make disciples.

When we make disciples, we have the potential to change the world. That's why it was said of Paul and his small band of co-laborers that they had turned the world upside down. They changed the world because they had been changed.

Light always dispels darkness. However, if we're not growing in the light, then we'll never be capable of dispelling darkness.

The Power of Discipleship and Evangelism

When we embrace the love and holiness of God as two wonderful aspects of the nature of Christ, we will grow into His image and place ourselves in a position of fulfilling God's original intent. When God's holiness and love are embraced simultaneously, they are incredibly powerful. The Multiplying Church Movement in Brazil has been so powerful because it built this balance into the foundation of its ministry. They have developed small groups for the purpose of making disciples and helping believers grow. However, outreach has been a major part of the small group experience. The small groups don't become comfortable with only having a nice Bible study that helps believers to grow. The small groups exist to make disciples with hearts to reach their family, friends, and colleagues.

The Brazilian Multiplying Church Movement has five major principles upon which it is built: 1) prayer, 2) discipleship and evangelism, 3) leadership training, 4) multiplying churches, and 5) showing compassion in the community. This balance is making a difference in communities throughout Brazil. They've impacted communities in the wealthiest suburbs as well as the poorest neighborhoods. They've seen explosive growth in churches that were ready to close their doors, and they started numerous new churches. They've won many thousands of people to Christ through small group discipleship.

As I write this manuscript, I'm working with the Multiplying Church Movement in Brazil to spread the concept of discipleship and evangelism to several nations. We have a major outreach, which will include training three million followers of Jesus around the world to share their faith with those whom they love—family, friends, and colleagues. All of this will be done through small discipleship groups. Everyone who comes to Christ will be immediately brought into a small group that will show the person how to grow in relationship with God. We plan to have evangelistic events to help mobilize the small discipleship groups to tell the good news of God's love to those they love. We are making disciples who will share Christ with families and friends. They will then help those who come to Christ to grow in their faith until they can do the same.

I've been overwhelmed with what I've seen through the Multiplying Church Movement. When we set our hearts to make disciples—who make disciples who make disciples—we are embarking on a road that can lead us to a great awakening among God's people. The potential is incredible. When we comprehend that today's tools enable us to fulfill the original intent of God in a much deeper and broader way than we've ever dreamed, we will fall to our knees and cry to God for the greatest revival the church has ever seen. Discipleship evangelism lies at the very heart of what Jesus told His disciples right before He ascended to the right hand of the Father.

Chapter 9
Multiplying Disciples through Innovation

~

But the word of God grew and multiplied. —Acts 12:24

When I spoke about discipleship evangelism at a conference for leaders of the Persian house church movement in Turkey, a pastor told
me, "Sammy, I live in Germany and work with the Persians there.
Could you come to Germany? We desperately need discipleship.
God is doing something that is completely unexpected. We need
your teaching on discipleship evangelism."

When I quizzed him about this move of God's Spirit, he explained.
"We have had about seventy people in attendance for many years.
However, some Afghan refugees showed up at our church a few
months ago. They said that they wanted to know more about Jesus.
I wasn't sure if they were trying to use Christianity to get a visa or if
they sincerely wanted to know about Jesus. I was a little skeptical but
shared the gospel with them. I told them about Jesus and the necessity of repentance and faith in Him. I told them that if they wanted to
follow Jesus, they could call upon His name and invite Jesus to take
control of their lives.

"They thanked me and left. The following Sunday, they returned
but brought more refugees with them. They said that they had
prayed as I had instructed them. God had answered their prayers,
and they wanted their friends to hear about Jesus. We proclaimed
the gospel to them, and they believed in Jesus. This has continued for
a few months, and we outgrew the German church we were renting
because so many people came to Christ."

The pastor showed me a video of a recent baptismal service he conducted. More than one hundred Afghan and Iranian refugees were baptized. These new believers cried, shouted "hallelujah," and embraced one another with joy. I knew these weren't people simply trying to obtain a visa into Europe. Something had happened in the hearts of these refugees. God was at work.

I agreed to go to Germany. Chill bumps covered my arms as I walked into the large German church. It reminded me of my days in East Germany during the times of communism. The church was packed with young people—this time from Afghanistan and Iran. I proclaimed Christ, and many responded in faith to the message and became followers of Jesus.

I also spent time speaking to the leaders of the church, teaching about discipleship. A young woman, who had not been in Germany very long, translated my teachings. However, she wept when we were introduced. I wasn't sure what was happening. Once she gained her composure, she told me, "When I became a believer in Tehran, I was so hungry to learn how to walk with God. The first Christian book in Persian that I ever read was your book, *The Prayer Factor*. You are like a spiritual father to me."

I was overwhelmed. After she translated my message that evening about the necessity of evangelism and discipleship, she told me that her family had visited her in Germany. She shared the gospel with them, and they also became followers of Jesus. After they returned to Iran, they led twenty-two other people in their family to Christ. She asked how she could help those family members grow in Christ. I shared some of the ways in which we were developing technology to enable people to cross borders to disciple their friends and families. She was thrilled at the possibility of using technology to help her extended family grow in their faith. She could make disciples in Iran, even though she lived in Germany.

A New Day for Multiplying Disciples

We live in one of the most exciting moments of history ever afforded the church. Two major streams of events have merged to provide the greatest opportunity the church has ever had to fulfill the original intent of God. Many of today's news broadcasts describe the grave dangers we face. Those dire threats are not to be taken lightly. Grave perils fill the world in which we live. Yet the very things that make the world dangerous create the same conditions that provide the greatest opportunity for the church to multiply disciples. However, the church must focus on the heavenly hope rather than the horrific hazards that stand before us.

Two strands of developments give us the possibility to fulfill God's original intent: movements of people around the world and the development of new technology. First, the world is within our reach because God has brought the world to the world. Second, because of new communication technology, we can virtually cross borders today that were previously impossible to traverse.

We must understand that God has given us a special moment in history. It's a new day. I traveled to Italy during the last couple of years to preach the gospel and also to train disciple makers. I can assure you that the vehicle I used to cross the Atlantic Ocean was not a ship with a lateen sail. Nor did I travel on the ancient Roman roads after I arrived in Rome. And it was not necessarily Christians who built the plane in which I flew. Nor was it believers who built the highways on which we drove. I never gave it a second thought to travel on a plane or on an Italian highway. That may seem like an exaggerated point to make. However, future generations may scratch their heads when they learn that many Christians didn't travel the new Roman road after it was built in order to fulfill the Great Commission of Christ.

Movements of People

When the refugee crisis in Europe first erupted in the media, Dr. Paul Negrut, rector of Emanuel University in Oradea, Romania, called me. The university is part of the fruit of the revival that took place in Romania during the days of communism, and Dr. Negrut was one of God's instruments during that awakening. He said, "Sammy, you and I know that these movements of people are not just political movements. We've experienced these historical moments and know that God is getting ready to do something wonderful. This is a special time. We must act—develop some kind of technology to reach the people with the gospel."

He was correct. As a result of that call, we partnered with the university to produce resources for discipleship and evangelism for the refugees in Europe. Dr. Negrut's call caused me to think about the movements of people around the world. We live in a historic time in which God has thrust people from all over the world into the rest of the world. I had lunch with the leader of a large mission agency in the United States who said,

"There's someone from every unreached people group in the world living in the United States."

Wow! Think about that. If he's accurate, then we have the potential to impact the world from our own local communities. If we could only see that there are thousands of people like the young Persian woman who translated for me in Germany. And they now live in our communities. Many of them are Christians, and others need to know the good news of God's love. God has placed many of them in our communities so that we might develop relationships with them and help them to know Christ, grow in Him, and share God's love with those back in their homelands.

I recently spoke to a pastor with a passion to reach the world with the gospel. However, he felt limited to what he could do because of the location of his church. After listening to him for several minutes, I discovered he had started two congregations of people from Myanmar. Each gathering came from a different tribal group and spoke a different language. I encouraged him, saying that God has given his church an incredible opportunity to reach an entire nation from its present location. He only needed to establish a strong relationship with the Myanmar believers, cast a vision for discipleship and evangelism, and partner with them to reach back to their homeland.

I spoke at a meeting of Persian Christians in a major city in the United States. A friend who lived in the city contacted me and said he would love to minister to the Persians in his city. He asked if I could arrange for him to speak to the Persian congregation. I told him the best approach was for me to make an introduction. He could then take the pastor out for coffee and begin to develop a relationship with him and his congregation. Most people from around the world whom God has brought to the Western world desire a relationship, not just a ministry opportunity. We need to develop and build those relationships. When we do, we will have the ability to minister to people in ways beyond anything we could have ever imagined.

We need to see the people whom God has sent to our communities and cities in the same way Jesus saw the people all around Him. The Bible tells us, "But when He saw the multitudes, He was moved with compassion for them, because they were weary and scattered, like sheep having no shepherd. Then He said to His disciples, 'The harvest truly is plentiful, but the laborers are few. Therefore pray the Lord of the harvest to send out laborers into His harvest'" (Matthew 9:36–38).

God has sent the multitudes to us. We need to see them through the eyes of Jesus. When we do, we will cry out to God to send harvesters into the harvest fields.

New Technology

God has provided this generation with communication tools that enable the church to cross borders that were once impossible and shatter language barriers that have kept people from knowing Christ and growing in their faith. These tools bridge the great generational divide and bring people together in wonderful ways.

Pastor Jolly of India and Pastor Fabricio of Brazil have desired to learn from the wisdom I've gained in more than fifty years of ministry. I've looked to them to understand how to effectively deliver the great truths of the Word of God to a new generation. They've taught me many lessons about technology. They've grown up with it. Social media is second nature to them.

The first lesson they taught me is never to depend on a particular technology. There are spiritual and practical reasons for this. First, our complete dependence must always be upon God. Once we begin to trust in the newest technology rather than God, our future is failure. We must always approach strategy from the position of prayer. Our reliance must always be upon God and not methods. That's not just spiritual rhetoric. It's an absolute necessity.

There are also other reasons we must never depend upon one technology. Technology changes rapidly, and old technology can quickly make our methods obsolete if we don't keep pace with the change. This is probably one of the greatest reasons my generation (baby boomers) doesn't attempt to use technology to reach the world with the gospel. We attempt such things as developing a website. Once it's completed, we want to sit back, relax, and consider the work is done. Yet our website's delivery methods and style will be outdated within a matter of a few years.

New and better ways of communication are being developed at such a rapid pace that it's mind-boggling. But we can't afford to drop out. My younger friends have been patient with me because they desire the wisdom my generation has to offer. However, their patience must be reciprocated. My generation must be willing to adapt. We must say with the Apostle Paul, "For I am already being poured out as a drink offering, and the time of my departure is at hand. I have fought the good fight, I have finished the race, I have kept the faith" (2 Timothy 4:6–7). We must live as dying men and women who have a message for a dying world. We cannot stop finding ways to share the gospel until we cross the finish line.

One of the greatest lessons that enabled me to reach people in ways I never would have imagined was to develop a toolbox and keep a variety of technology tools in it. At the moment of this writing, I regularly use Facebook, WhatsApp, websites, Skype, Zoom, YouTube, Vimeo, Messenger, and FaceTime. Each one of those tools provides a different function. For instance, I have used the video chat services, Skype and Zoom, to preach large evangelistic outreaches and disciple believers around the world. I was able to disciple and train leaders in Pakistan while my interpreter spoke simultaneously from Sweden. I placed a green screen behind me. He sent a photo of his background, and I was able to make my background identical to his. We then placed our video images side by side. Thus, it gave the feel of our being together as he translated for me. I've used the same approach for creating discipleship materials for Swahili speakers in East Africa.

Some of you may wonder why I haven't mentioned other great technology tools. I only use a tool when I fully understand how it can help fulfill my mission—the fulfillment of God's original intent. We don't need to run after every new gadget or technology tool that has been created. We need to determine exactly what God wants us to do. Then we find the tool or tools that help us accomplish that task.

That's exactly what my friend, Dr. Wade Akins, did. He observed what I was doing and asked me to teach him how to do the same thing. Even though he wanted to reach people for Christ and train Christian leaders, he worked with an entirely different set of circumstances. He implemented what I taught him and used the specific technology tools that enabled him to accomplish his mission. He didn't copy what I did. He found the tools in the toolbox that helped him accomplish what God had given him to do. And it has been incredibly effective.

Technology, Revival, and God's Intent

Who are the dreamers of this generation? Where are the intercessors seeking God for a mighty revival? Who will bow down and worship the King and then rise up and proclaim the gospel? Who will ask God for innovative ways to fulfill His original intent?

We stand on the cusp of one of the greatest moments in the history of the church. It's decision time. We can squander the moment or we can cry out to God and ask Him to pour out His Spirit among His people. We must leave our comfort zones, place our feet on the modern-day Roman roads, and go! A twenty-first century revival will transport us to people and cultures that may seem strange. It will cause us to love people as we've never loved them. It will enable us to see the words of Jesus fulfilled: "And this gospel of the kingdom will be preached in all the world as a witness to all the nations, and then the end will come" (Matthew 24:14).

God has not changed. His original intent has never been altered. God's heart remains faithful. Will we be faithful? He is the Creator. Will we become creative? Jesus wept. Do we weep? Jesus made disciples who made disciples. What are we doing?

Afterword

~

After completing this manuscript, I concluded the most extensive discipleship/evangelism plan of action I have ever undertaken. I partnered with my friends mentioned in this book to train Christians to pray for and share Jesus with their family and friends. We established discipleship groups in eleven languages throughout sixty-eight countries by using WhatsApp, Facebook, satellite television, and YouTube.

We used the digital discipleship groups not only to equip Christians to share the gospel but also to follow up on new believers who would place their faith in Jesus. It began with a dream, which Pastor Fabricio and the Multiplying Church Movement leaders had in Brazil during May 2019. Friends in India, Pakistan, and Iran quickly adopted the strategy.

We didn't know that COVID-19 was on its way and would confine billions of people to their homes. The virus forced people around the world to communicate with one another through social media and communication technology tools such as WhatsApp and Facebook. Our small band of Christian leaders scattered across the globe were positioned to reach many of those people with the gospel.

Hurting people around the world came across our Facebook evangelistic event in their news feed. A woman living in Amritsar, India, contacted Pastor Jolly after watching the Facebook presentation. She had been depressed and considered suicide before she watched the livestream evangelistic event. She gave her heart to Christ and told Pastor Jolly and his team that she had found hope. A man in Brazil was also contemplating suicide when he came across the livestream program in Portuguese. He gave his heart to Christ and was immediately brought into a discipleship group to help him to grow in Christ. Two medical personnel in India were afraid to go to work because of COVID-19. After listening to the gospel, they gave their hearts to Christ and had the courage to return to work. Testimonies like this abounded from multiple nations.

More than fifteen million people viewed the evangelistic event. Our ministry started 1,500 small discipleship groups in sixty-eight countries. Pastor Jolly and his team started hundreds of small discipleship groups in India via WhatsApp. The Multiplying Church Movement of Brazil reported that 20,000 Christian leaders downloaded the discipleship and training materials. A Christian satellite television network for Iran created discipleship and evangelism training programs, using the strategy and principles outlined in this book.

My hope is that the Christian church will do much more than simply livestream their Sunday morning services. My prayer is that Christians will dream, pray, and devise a strategy to multiply disciples by using the tools that God has given this generation. We must make disciples, who will make disciples, who will also make disciples!

**If you enjoyed this book,
will you consider sharing the message with others?**

Let us know your thoughts at info@ironstreammedia.com.
You can also let the author know by visiting or sharing a photo of the
cover on our social media pages or leaving a review at a retailer's site.
All of it helps us get the message out!

Facebook.com/IronStreamMedia

———————

Iron Stream Books, New Hope® Publishers, Ascender Books, and
New Hope Kidz are imprints of Iron Stream Media, which derives its
name from Proverbs 27:17,
"As iron sharpens iron, so one person sharpens another."

This sharpening describes the process of discipleship, one to
another. With this in mind, Iron Stream Media provides a variety of
solutions for churches, ministry leaders, and nonprofits ranging from
in-depth Bible study curriculum and Christian book publishing to
custom publishing and consultative services. Through our popular
Life Bible Study, Student Life Bible Study brands, and New Hope
imprints, ISM provides web-based full-year and short-term Bible
study teaching plans as well as printed devotionals, Bibles, and
discipleship curriculum.

For more information on ISM and Iron Stream Books, please visit

IronStreamMedia.com

Printed in the United States
By Bookmasters